D0389363

CONTINENTS OF EXILE

THE RED LETTERS

Mamaji and Daddyji. Simla. 1934.

VED MEHTA

CONTINENTS OF EXILE

THE RED LETTERS

MY FATHER'S ENCHANTED PERIOD

Nation Books
New York

THE RED LETTERS: *My Father's Enchanted Period*

Published by

AVALON
publishing group incorporated

Nation Books
An Imprint of Avalon Publishing Group
245 W. 17th St., 11th Floor
New York, NY 10011

Nation Books is a co-publishing venture of the Nation Institute and Avalon Publishing Group Incorporated.

Library of Congress Cataloging-in-Publication Data is available
Photographs on pages 74 and 75 by Samuel Bourne

ISBN 1-56025-628-1

10 9 8 7 6 5 4 3 2 1

Printed in the United States of America
Distributed by Publishers Group West

In Memory of William Cary and to Katherine Cary

CONTENTS

———————————

PHOTOGRAPHS

CONTINENTS OF EXILE

THE RED LETTERS

PROLOGUE

THE LONG SHADOW

ON THE PARTY

I N 1967, MY YOUNGER SISTER, USHA, WAS EXPECTING her first child in Charleston, South Carolina, where her American husband, a lieutenant in the Navy, was temporarily stationed. My mother was determined to be with Usha for her confinement, as she had been with my three older sisters for their confinements in India. The fact that Usha was living in Charleston, thousands of miles away from New Delhi, where my parents lived, seemed to be an obstacle for my mother only in terms of money, something she'd always understood and managed well. Indeed, it was a matter of pride with her that, in spite of my father's meagre government salary as an Indian public-health official and his openhanded ways, she had been able to keep all seven of us children in respectable clothes and respectable shoes as we were growing up. Fortunately, near the time of Usha's confinement, my father, who was now in his early seventies and had long since retired from government service, got a medical assignment in New York City with a wealthy, eccentric, elderly

American patient of his, Mrs. Ethel Clyde, whom he had attended off and on for many years. She generally compensated him in an unconventional way—by buying his round-trip air ticket from New Delhi, taking care of his expenses while he was in America, and giving him a small stipend. The arrangement suited him; he was able to see me in New York, where I was living, and the stipend, nothing much in American terms, went some ways toward defraying his expenses in India. Assuming that the cost of my mother's lodging in America would be minimal, since most of the time she would be staying with Usha, he decided to splurge the stipend on another air ticket, for my mother, and bring her out with him.

My mother stopped briefly in New York on her way to Charleston, and eager to introduce my parents to some of the people who were closest to me in New York, I arranged a dinner party for them in my apartment. I invited William Shawn, the editor-in-chief of *The New Yorker*, who edited my writing; his wife, Cecille, and their two grown sons, Wallace and Allen; and my friend and amanuensis, Gwyneth Cravens. Despite tremendous good will all around, I expected the evening to be difficult. I was bringing together the two men who had had the greatest influence on me—my father and Mr. Shawn. After I had gone blind, two months short of my fourth birthday, everyone at home thought that my father should plan for a modest life for me, like that of a small-time shopkeeper, but my father never faltered in his ambition that I should aspire to the highest intellectual attainments. Later, in my middle twenties, when I was completing my nine years of college and university and was thrashing about for a means of earning my living, Mr. Shawn had opened up the vocational path of a writer to me. Indeed, since I had come to New York he had served in loco parentis, and I had developed an enormous amount of affection and regard for him. I wanted the two men to admire each other as I admired each of them. Yet I was all too aware of how vast the gulf that divided them was. My father was worldly; Mr. Shawn was otherworldly. My father thrived on the social stage, a sine qua non of his medical profession; Mr. Shawn mostly worked from behind the scenes, invisibly improving and perfecting other people's writing and art work, and usually avoided all social engagements not directly connected with his work. I thought it was a great mark of his affection for me that he had agreed to come to the party.

My anxiety was compounded by the fact that my mother spoke broken English, and Mrs. Shawn, except for a jaunt in Europe, had scarcely stirred out of Chicago and New York; the two of them would be forced to communicate mostly through nonverbal expressions of warmth. No doubt Wallace would help interpret; he had stayed with my parents in New Delhi a couple of years earlier, when he had been in India as a Fulbright scholar, but since leaving India he had fallen out of touch with them. Allen and Gwyn had had no direct contact with my parents or with India.

I lived in a small one-bedroom apartment, and there was hardly any space to move around. My living room was crammed with a sofa, easy chairs, and a long dining table and dining chairs—furniture I had bought for a much larger apartment when I was in my twenties, in my more expansionist days. The party would be cozy and intimate, but the obverse side of that was that there would be no buffer of other people—no place to hide in case of social awkwardness. The evening had the potential to collapse like a soufflé.

To my relief, the party got off to a good start. My parents cut graceful, impressive figures, with my mother in a beautiful silk sari and my father in an elegant tweed jacket. He was chatty, while she used smiles, gestures, and hugs to good effect. The Shawns, as always, were warm and outgoing, and Gwyn was a wonderful moral support.

Then, just when I thought everything was going fine, my father said, as if in a desperate conversational gambit to Mr. Shawn, "You have wonderful jokes in your magazine."

I squirmed. I had become so hypersensitive to language under Mr. Shawn's editing that my father's slight linguistic misfire—saying "jokes" when he meant "cartoons"—embarrassed me.

But Mr. Shawn seemed instinctively to understand that my father was anxious. He laughed graciously and asked, "Do those jokes really make sense all the way over in India?"

"Yes, sir," my father said. "We Punjabis especially like a good joke—we like to laugh a lot."

"That's fascinating," Mr. Shawn said. "I wonder why that is."

To my horror, my father launched into a lecture about the Punjabis—their character, their habits, their language—leaving Mr. Shawn's simple question far behind. I was mortified. I wished I could tell my father that there was no need for him to try to impress Mr. Shawn with his store of knowledge about Punjabis. Ordinarily, he was able to manage a conversation with almost anyone, but because he knew how I revered Mr. Shawn he was going all out to dazzle him. But then I reminded myself that many of us writers were also anxious to have Mr. Shawn's good opinion—indeed, involuntarily behaved around him like schoolboys in front of their esteemed headmaster.

Mr. Shawn listened with unwavering attention. That was his way—always trying to connect with what someone was feeling or thinking or interested in, putting aside his own views and preconceptions.

As the evening went on, my father, if anything, became more voluble. I attributed that in part to his having had a couple of glasses of wine. He had been a teetotaller for most of his life and hadn't touched alcohol until he was in his late fifties, and then took only a few sips of whiskey or brandy medicinally, because of a heart attack he had had a year earlier.

At one point, when I was offering around ginger ale and wine, I overheard my father say to Gwyn, in a surprisingly choked and maudlin voice, "As a medical man, I can tell you that eighty-five per cent of information is taken in through the eyes. Ved somehow manages to take all of that information in through his ears. Isn't that remarkable?"

He's not behaving like his usual, circumspect self, I thought. He may be hoping to elicit Gwyn's admiration for me, but without knowing it he is inviting her to pity me. That goes against everything that I stand for. It's not like him to be so insensitive. But then there was no way I could control him and, anyway, if he sounded simultaneously proud and sad that was to be expected. After all, the only blind people he ever came across in India were destitute beggars stumbling around with sticks and begging bowls.

As I was pouring some ginger ale for the Shawns (they were all teetotallers), my father called me over and asked for some brandy.

I didn't want to get into an argument with him, especially with the Shawns present, so I got a snifter and poured him some brandy. Perhaps my hand shook. In any case, I poured more of it than I meant to.

"Are you feeling all right?" I asked my father in Punjabi, handing him the snifter.

"Never better," he said, emphasizing "never," as if he sensed that I didn't like his talking so much and were trying to cover up his own embarrassment. Since my childhood, we had been so close that he was quick to pick up on every slight change in my feelings—even experiencing them as his own.

Soon I was busy checking on dinner, which was being prepared by a hired cook, and getting hors d'oeuvres and ice. In any event, I made a point of not being within earshot of my father, thinking that, that way, he would feel less anxious and act more like himself.

As the guests rose to serve themselves dinner, my father first got a plate, then put it down again, without having served himself, saying in Punjabi, "Son, I'm not feeling well, and I need to lie down."

My spirits sank.

My mother said to me in Punjabi, "You continue with your hostly duties. I'll put Doctor Sahib to bed." Both of them disappeared into the little bedroom.

"My father hardly ever drinks," I said to the room, my voice sounding rather forlorn to my ears.

"I know," Mr. Shawn said, as if he had taken in everything.

"Let's face it," Wallace said. "People often feel sick at parties. I do all the time."

Allen laughed out loud, as if to say that no one had the capacity for enjoying a party more than his brother did.

Mrs. Shawn started to contradict Wallace, but halfway into her sentence seemed to realize that she had all but impaled herself on the horns of a dilemma: if she flatly contradicted him, she would be casting aspersions on my father's behavior, but if she agreed with him, she would be making Wallace himself sound like someone who couldn't handle social situations. She ended up not completing the sentence and covering her confusion with a laugh of her own.

Mr. Shawn started edging toward the door but then, realizing that we hadn't yet had dinner, came back and courteously sat down while Mrs. Shawn prepared a plate for him. Gwyn and I served ourselves and found places to sit. Everyone seemed to relax a little with the food.

In the middle of dinner, Gwyn excused herself to go to the bathroom.

Later, she told me, "When I stood up, I didn't realize that there was no way to get to the bathroom without walking through the bedroom, but there was nothing to be done. I gingerly opened the bedroom door. Your father was lying face down diagonally across the bed, with his tweed jacket on the floor. I noticed the beautiful satin lining on it. Your mother saw me looking at it, picked it up, and laid it over your father with such tenderness, with such a sweet expression of devotion and kindness on her face, that I felt like an intruder. Still, I am glad I witnessed the moment. It will always stay with me."

When Gwyn rejoined the party and my mother still hadn't come out to have her dinner, I stepped into the bedroom and was aghast to discover that my father was sobbing on the bed.

I sent my mother back to the living room, and I sat down on the edge of the bed and took his hand. He was shaking all over.

"I'll be all right," he said through his sobs. "I just need a little time." Soon, he fell asleep.

As if to spare me embarrassment, people went home without his ever having emerged. Their quick departure was a bit like a lunch I once had with some friends in a restaurant. We were barely settling down to our dessert when the maître d' went around the room banging on a platter and announcing that the restaurant had received a bomb threat. The room emptied so quickly it was hard to imagine that a minute before it had been humming with activity. I never knew where the threat had come from or how serious it had been; I just had a vague feeling of having been a witness to an occasion abruptly interrupted.

When I saw Gwyn at the office the morning after the dinner party, I said to her, "I was quite confused at the strange turn things took last night. What do you think happened?"

"I was puzzled myself," she said. "I couldn't have imagined a nicer group of people, and yet everything seemed to go awry."

We did what we often did with a messy draft of writing—tried to put the material in some kind of an order.

"What happened after I gave my father the brandy?" I asked.

"He seemed to drink it quickly. He started talking about your accomplishments with a great deal of fatherly pride. Then without any warning, he shifted into a stream of self-accusations, but not at all in a maudlin, drunken way. He seemed suddenly to drop his social mask and to speak from the heart. His suffering was evident. He said he had always felt responsible for what he called the tragedy of your blindness—how he blamed himself for not acting promptly when you got sick. Though he suspected you had meningitis, he delayed by a day driving you to a hospital, where you could be properly diagnosed and treated. I said something reassuring, but without pausing he went on to explain the reason for his delay. He had

7

arranged a tennis party at the local club for a visiting English superior that evening. He wanted to please the superior because he was hoping to firm up a pending promotion. He said he could have backed out, but there were conflicting diagnoses of your illness, and the hospital was seventy miles away in Lahore, so he procrastinated. He thought that his delay had been fateful. He was convinced that, if he had acted on his hunch, cancelled the tennis party, and had you tested and treated for meningitis at the hospital, he might have saved your eyes."

I could scarcely take in what Gwyn was telling me. I was hearing for the first time the details that almost thirty years earlier had led up to my blindness. Until that moment, all I had known was that I had been stricken with cerebrospinal meningitis and that the fever had permanently damaged my optic nerves. I had grown up attaching no more significance to my blindness than I did to the fact that one of my legs had always been a little shorter than the other. Anyway, I could hardly believe that my father had chosen a near-stranger as his confidant, and that at a party.

"I'm hearing this for the first time, Gwyn," I said. "What an uncomfortable situation for you to be put in! I wish I had had some sense of what was going on, so that I could have deflected him. Where was I when he was saying all this to you? Too busy getting drinks? I am appalled that Mr. Shawn had to listen to such personal stuff. What must he have thought of my father?"

"I don't think any of the Shawns heard a thing. You know how discreet they are. They just kept talking among themselves."

"I wonder why he chose you to unburden himself. I know you come across as sympathetic, but that can't be the whole explanation."

"Maybe it was because he saw that I was pregnant and would soon have a child of my own. Anyway, I think he knew that as your amanuensis I was close to you, and from the beginning he was solicitous of me. He made me sit next to him. Also, it might have been easier for him to confide in a virtual stranger than in someone he knew. I tried to console him by telling him that you thought he had been a great father to you, but that made him more upset. He became emotional. Tears came into his eyes."

"But I don't understand, Gwyn. He was seeing me in the best possible situation. I was in command. I had fulfilled his expectations, my own expectations, of living by myself in my own apartment, entertaining like anyone else, earning my own living—of being independent. That should have been a joyous occasion for him."

Even as I said this, I realized that, no matter what I accomplished, how comfortable I felt with myself, for him nothing could compensate for the loss of my eyesight. That was the Indian attitude—my mother's attitude and, for all my father's Western education and professions of enlightened opinions, his, too, it seemed. If so, his watching me managing things so well at the party might have only underscored for him what I was lacking. He might have even pitied me, much as he sometimes pitied someone at bridge who valiantly struggled with a weak hand, only to lose in the end. But such thoughts were soon overwhelmed by a surge of interest I felt about the circumstances leading up to my blindness. Until then, I had had no inkling that my father had played a role in it, and perhaps a crucial one. But I resisted believing that a day's delay, whether advertent or inadvertent, could have made any difference.

Later, when I was with my parents, I asked my father about that and also how it was that he felt in any way responsible for my blindness.

Before he could answer, my mother said, under her breath, "Leave it. It is bad luck to talk about such things."

I turned to my father, but he did not seem able to add anything substantial to what Gwyn had already passed on to me. I told him that the time for him to tell me the circumstances of my blindness would have been when I was writing my first book, a youthful autobiography, thirteen years earlier.

"It didn't strike me then that it was part of your story," he said. "If I thought about it at all, I must have concluded that it was part of my story."

I didn't pursue the subject. How I went blind, though no doubt of biographical interest, had no relevance to my emotional present, I thought at that time. My blindness was a fait accompli, and my regretting it would be rather like regretting that I wasn't a musician or a politician. "If"s and "can"s are fun to dream about, but they have nothing to do with present reality. Still, I continued to be haunted by the image of him lying face down on my bed, sobbing for my loss and blaming himself for it when he should have been rejoicing in my self-reliance, for which I often thought I had only his unflagging encouragement to thank.

Three or four years later, I found myself doing research into my father's life, which resulted in my writing and publishing a book about him entitled "Daddyji," the first of a series of books, independent but connected, of which this is the last. In "Daddyji" I was forced to review minutely every last detail leading up to my blindness, including my mother's part in it: she had tired me out with a long walk in the cold just hours before the onset of the fever, and she blamed herself for that, much as my father blamed himself for his tennis party. The book also allowed my father and mother to talk freely to me, for the first time, about their individual memories of the event. It thereby went some measure toward reconciling perhaps them, and certainly me, to the irrelevance of the tantalizing might-have-beens to the reality of my blindness. But it would not lay to rest the spectre of my father sobbing guiltily on my bed in the middle of the party—a spectre that turned out to have many more ramifications and layers of meaning than I had ever imagined.

I

HILL GIRLS AND PRINCELINGS

I N 1961, SIX YEARS BEFORE THE ILL-FATED PARTY, I had left my graduate studies at Harvard and moved to New York at the age of twenty-six to try to make my living as a writer. I had barely settled in when my father arrived in the city, to attend to Mrs. Clyde. My apartment at the time was one L-shaped room on East Fifty-eighth Street, and so it suited both of us that he should stay, as he usually did, in Mrs. Clyde's apartment at 1 Fifth Avenue. But we met often for meals and talks; sometimes during the day he would camp out in my apartment, waiting for me to come home from my office at *The New Yorker*, where I had just become a staff writer.

One Saturday morning, while I was waiting to have lunch with my father, I took my shoes to the cobbler around the corner for new heels. I had barely entered his shop when he jumped up from his stitching machine and came around the counter.

"Mr. Mehta!" he said, exuberantly taking both my hands.

I stiffened. I scarcely knew the fellow. How dare he be so

familiar with me? But then I worried that I was being unnecessarily standoffish. After all, he was like a neighbor.

"I have a copy of your book. I am in the middle of reading it. It's wonderful."

"Really?" I said, somewhat flustered. Publicly owning up to the fact that I was a writer always made me shy. "Which book?" I asked him. I had published two.

" 'Face to Face.' "

I squirmed. That book was the autobiography, which had mostly been written when I was twenty and had been speaking English for just five years (it was completed when I was twenty-two). Now that I was embarking on a career as a serious writer, I disowned it. But then I realized that the cobbler wouldn't have cared what kind of English the book was written in—he himself spoke in a thick Polish accent—and that I should be flattered that he liked it.

But then he said, to my horror, "Your daddy, he inscribed the book for me and my missus."

It was one of my father's engaging qualities that he was comfortable talking to anyone and everyone, whether a cobbler or a prime minister. He had but to meet a stranger and he was apt to pull out pictures of our mother and us seven children and boast extravagantly about our achievements, as if he were a father in the small village of his boyhood rather than a well-travelled, cosmopolitan doctor. He was constantly ordering copies of my books from the publisher. No doubt it was one of these that he had presented to the cobbler, signing it, with a proud flourish, with his customary inscription: "Daddyji, author's father and character in the book."

I mumbled some inane thanks and hurried out. I was exasperated with my father and grew even more so when I met with a similar reception from the laundress at the laundromat and the pharmacist at the pharmacy, both of whom also had new copies of "Face to Face." Although doubtless my father had only been taking pride in me, still I felt that he wasn't acknowledging that I was now twenty-six years old, out of the sheltering environment of schools and universities and earning my own livelihood. He was acting as if I were still a dependent child, whom he could show off like a monkey on a chain. This was especially galling because I liked the thought of being anonymous in a big city and I felt that he had made it embarrassing for me to walk around in my own neighborhood.

Over lunch, I confronted him.

"I thought these nice people would like to read about you and our family and know the kind of background we come from," he said. "It's important to have good relations with your neighbors."

"But you really must stop inscribing the books."

"What harm is there in it? I knew you'd never do it."

I could never be indignant with my father for long, and soon we were laughing about what the cobbler and the laundress and the pharmacist would make of my sister Pom's wedding or my mother's Hindu superstitions.

"Only in New York would you find a cobbler who enjoys reading a book," my father said, then added, as if he were now making an effort to be casual, "You know, son, long before you became a writer, I was dreaming of becoming a novelist."

"You don't mean it."

"Yes, I do. What's more, I may surprise you, son, by writing a best-seller one of these days."

As far as I knew, he had never written anything except letters and medical reports, so privately I dismissed his aspirations as just talk. Aloud, I said, "Best-sellers look easy-to-write and formulaic, but even accomplished writers have trouble bringing them off." He was in one of his optimistic moods, though, and nothing I said seemed to quiet his spirits.

After that, whenever we met, he would bring up again the subject of his writing a novel. Still, I did not pay it much mind, because he had always been something of a dreamer, a little like Mr. Micawber in "David Copperfield." Whenever I went to parties, I was sure to meet a woman who would tell me that her daughter wrote such beautiful letters from her school

that she felt someone should collect and publish them. I sometimes thought that, if I stood at the front of a Fifth Avenue bus
and asked those passengers who were writers to raise their
hands, every hand would go up.

Six years had passed since my embarrassing encounter with
the cobbler. I was now thirty-three, and my father was seventy-
two. He was again in New York, this time with my mother for
Usha's confinement.

"As you know, son, procrastination is my worst habit," he
said during one of his visits to my apartment, after my mother
had left to be with Usha in Charleston. "But I have now
engaged a good steno in New Delhi and am finally getting
down to the job of writing. Once I get back home, I'll send you
something."

Again I didn't take his project seriously. By now I had published three more books, and I thought that I might have
unwittingly stirred up a spirit of competition in him.

Anyway, after he returned home I heard nothing more
about the novel. Then, several months later, I received a draft
of its first chapter, with a note asking me to rewrite it for him,
saying, "After all, son, I'm a medical man, and I don't have the
vinegar and spice that authors like you use to make your stories interesting."

From the draft, it was clear that he had a gift for telling a
story. I should have been able to foresee that—any time he was
describing an incident to listeners he would command their
full attention. Indeed, I had sometimes thought my own pen-
chant for writing stories might have come from him. Still, as
he himself realized, his writing style was more suited to a government report than to narrative fiction; instead of dialogue,
for example, the chapter had summaries of dialogue. But I
found the material fascinating, and I set about rewriting it. In
time, we hit upon a method for what turned into a father-son
collaboration. He would send me some rough notes from New
Delhi, and I would write them up in New York and send him
the draft. He would then go over the draft, expand it and offer

new ideas, and send it back to me for yet another rewrite. In this way, we exchanged as many as a dozen drafts over a year or two. As much as possible, I tried to keep to the spirit of his ideas, though the details were filtered through and embellished by my imagination. At first I took up the task as a way of keeping in touch with him, even, perhaps, humoring him. I found it diverting from the serious writing I did every day. Certainly, the story he wanted to tell was not one I would have ever thought up, myself. It seemed like a fairy tale—superficially magical, but with dark undertones—yet its deeper structure revealed itself to me only gradually. Anyway, once I got involved in it I couldn't drop it, especially after it began to acquire a certain foreboding significance in our relationship— but more about that, in due course. What follows is the result of our joint effort, to which we gave the title "Hill Girls and Princelings."

❧

As a boy, Chander had a talent for drawing and mathematics, and he wanted to grow up to be an engineer. But his father wanted him to be a doctor.

"It's better to spend your time saving our poor people from plague and cholera than building monuments to the British," his father would say. Chander, being a good son, joined the King Edward Medical College in Lahore. During his first summer vacation, to escape the heat, he went on a trek up in Kangra district, in the Punjab Himalayas. He was nineteen and restless, full of energy and curiosity.

Chander had hardly climbed his first hill when he spotted an isolated shack set on an incongruously beautiful site. He walked up and peeped in through the little open window. An old man was mixing some powders by its light, and he looked up.

"You seem to be new to these parts, young man. Can I help you?" The old man's voice wafted out, clear, if distant.

"I was thinking that there was something I could do to help you," said Chander, on impulse, walking into the shack.

The old man introduced himself as the hillside's only medical man, the compounder who mixed medicines for the local dispensary, for that is what the shack was. He resumed his mixing.

Thinking that helping the compounder at the rural dispensary for the summer would be a good way to get some experience while exploring the hills, Chander told him that he was a medical student and offered his services.

"I couldn't afford to pay you," warned the compounder. "I myself just get by."

"Plain food and a roof over my head are all I need," Chander said, eager to be accommodating.

The old man sealed the bargain by stepping up to the young man and embracing him.

One of Chander's first patients was a pale, thin girl. She had bright, greenish-blue eyes and a loosely coiled long braid of golden hair, which she nervously twisted while Chander was taking down her medical history. He noticed that she had the developed figure of someone older than her twelve years.

"Tell me what your symptoms are," he said, but he couldn't get her to say anything.

The plump woman who had brought the girl there gave her a push and said, "Reshmi is always complaining of being run-down. That's just her way of avoiding work. Just give her some medicine to make her strong."

Chander noticed that the girl had malar flush, jotted it down in her history, counted out some quinine and iron tablets, and told the woman to see that the girl took the medicine and got more to eat. He was sure that the woman, and the well-fed six-year-old boy whom she had also brought along, were eating their fill at the expense of the girl.

Throughout the day, every time one patient left two more arrived, but Chander could not get the pale girl with the golden hair out of his head.

In the evening, he made some inquiries about that small family and was directed to their hut on a nearby hillock. Through the open door, he could see heaps of fleece tied in loose bundles stacked to the ceiling. The musty smell coming out of the hut was so overwhelming that he had to step back. There was no sign of the pale girl with the golden hair, but the plump woman was there and, spotting him, she came out.

"I was passing by and I saw you, so I thought I'd stop and see how the girl is doing," Chander said. "Where is she?"

"She's tending to the sheep on the lea. She'll be back before long."

Chander sat down on a rock next to a small stream with a trickle of water in it, while the woman stood scowling beside him with her arms akimbo.

"In monsoon season that stream becomes flooded," she said. "It gets so full that you can't even cross to the lea. Sometimes it floods the house. Then we have to move out and sleep wherever we can find shelter."

She gave him a pitiful glance, as if she were hoping for a handout. But, looking at her standing there, plump as a setting hen, Chander recalled the well-fed boy and the pale, thin girl and could feel little sympathy for the woman.

He gestured at the bundles in the hut, and said pointedly, "Those must bring you a good bit of money."

"Not nearly enough, sahib. My husband and I do our best, but we've got four mouths to feed, and the hill winters are severe."

Just then, Chander caught sight of the girl and a man bringing home the flock of sheep. The woman beckoned the girl over, handed her a piece of dry bread, and ordered her to go put the sheep in the pen. Chander thought that the girl wanted to linger, but she promptly obeyed.

"She needs more nourishment than that," Chander said hotly. "You should feed—"

"I am very fond of my daughter," the man broke in. He spoke Hindi with a pronounced Nepalese accent (he was of the

Gurkha tribe). "I am determined to get her away from her step-mother"—he pointed at the woman—"before she starves my poor Reshmi to death. She is always giving Reshmi's food to our son. She can't spoil him enough."

The woman protested peevishly: "He and his daughter go out from morning to night. They leave me here to bundle up the fleece, and cook and sew and clean and mend."

"The woman won't rest until I get the girl out of the house," the man said. He and his wife both carried on as if the other were not there, and seemed to be appealing to Chander for arbitration. "Even today, I was talking about Reshmi with the agents who recruit girls for the harem of the Nawab," he continued. "No doubt she would be better off in the harem of the Jat Raja in the upper hills, but the agents are much more liberal with the Nawab's money. I am a poor widower who must get the best price for my daughter." He spread his hands in a show of despair.

Chander was incensed. He had vaguely heard that the princelings' agents roamed the hills looking for desirable can-didates for the harems, but could not believe that young girls could be bought and sold like sheep right under the nose of the British, who prided themselves on stamping out "barbaric native customs." He seethed with anger at the stepmother and the father, at the princelings and the British authorities. His anger was tempered by a certain sympathy for the poor illit-erate shepherd, but Chander said to him sternly, "If you discuss the girl with an agent again, I will report you to the deputy commissioner, and the Englishman will put you in jail."

The shepherd quickly did an about-face. "Whoever said that I will sell my precious girl?" he said ingratiatingly. "I just said that to placate her stepmother, so that she will give my Reshmi enough food to fill her stomach."

"I always feed Reshmi as much as she deserves," the woman said. "Didn't I bring her to the dispensary today for medicine?"

Chander felt confused and frustrated. He thought he had never seen a more wretched family. He despaired of doing anything for them, and the overpowering smell of fleece was making him sick, so he mumbled his *namastes* and left.

❦

IN THE EVENINGS, after Chander had finished his work at the rural dispensary, he would hike into the hills and watch the hill girls tending sheep, fetching water, and slapping together straw and dung into patties to fuel their fires. Like Reshmi, many of them were pale and beautiful, and some of them were even quite saucy, tossing their long braids or throwing little smiles in his direction. Wherever he went, he heard more stories from villagers about such girls being sold off to one of the princelings—the Muslim Nawab or the Hindu Jat Raja.

Though Chander never so much as caught a glimpse of the Nawab himself, he did often see his motorcar cruising up and down the slopes. The car was furnished with tulle curtains, which allowed the passengers to see out but prevented anyone from seeing in. The Nawab's minions put it about that the car's passengers were the begums, but it was generally known that the royal lecher himself was inside, trawling for prospective recruits for his harem. Sometimes, the Nawab's agent, usually a mullah, would jump out of the car, accost the young village girl who apparently had caught the Nawab's fancy, tempt her with shining gold bangles or necklaces on the spot, hustle her into the car, and spirit her away. In order to keep the matter hushed up, away from the notice of the police and the British authorities, the agent would call on the parents under the cover of darkness later on and make an appropriate payment. Chander was at once disturbed and fascinated. Then he heard that the Nawab's mullah would regularly go around from hamlet to hamlet, preaching the message of Allah, using the Nawab's largesse to win converts and, at the same time, sizing up the village girls, most of whom had not yet reached puberty, as prospective recruits for the Nawab's harem. Whenever the mullah came to know about a real beauty, he filled the ears of her parents with lofty talk about the power of Islam, the strict observance of devout purdah in the Nawab's household, and the Nawab's generosity in running a "boarding school" for girls on the grounds of the luxurious palace. The parents were taken in by the religious talk, something that served as a salve to their conscience for accepting the Nawab's proffered money. The girl soon found herself in the harem instead of the supposed boarding school, never to be seen or heard of by her parents again.

Chander sought out the mullah, who tended the mosque near the Nawab's palace on the top of a hill, and gained the mullah's confidence by reciting the short Qalma that he had learned as a boy.

"Aren't you using religion for the profane purposes of the Nawab?" Chander asked the mullah eventually.

"I'm converting infidels to Islam," the mullah retorted.

Chander pointed out that the girls were minors and that taking them away from their homes was against the British law.

The mullah promptly replied that the authority of the Koran was higher than the British law and that the Koran made no distinction between minors and grown women. Moreover, he said that the Nawab not only got young girls for his boarding school but also got young boys to serve in his household. "The boys are trained to make carpets with the name of Allah woven into the pattern," the mullah said smoothly and slyly. "Thus, even as they are doing worldly work for the Nawab they are also doing heavenly work for Allah."

One day the compounder invited Chander to go with him to the Nawab's palace to meet His Highness himself, making no secret of the fact that even he received a handsome stipend from the palace for keeping an eye out for desirable young girls.

Chander chastised the old man for being no better than the mullah.

"I'm just a small fry," he answered. "I have no choice but to stay on the good side of the high and the mighty. What can someone like me do when even the big sahibs, like the British Civil Surgeon, wine and dine with His Highness?"

So His Highness uses religion to seduce girls, money to keep their parents silent, and lavish hospitality to traduce British authorities, Chander thought. He felt disgusted and angry.

"I will have nothing to do with such a scoundrel, however rich and powerful he might be," Chander said.

"Then you'd better quit this place quickly, before the Nawab gets a wind of your nosing around," the compounder said, sounding fatherly.

Chander took the compounder's warning to heart and in due course quit the Nawab's jurisdiction, together with the dispensary job. He could not, however, bring himself to leave the hills and go immediately back to Lahore. So he hired a mule and rode to the palace of the Jat Raja to snoop around there and to discover if he had any more scruples than the Nawab had. He never got past the gates of the Jat Raja's palace, but he did gather some provocative information from the villagers in this Highness's jurisdiction—that the Hindu princeling was as venal as his Muslim counterpart but that, unlike the girls in the Nawab's harem, who grew old and often died there, the girls in the Jat Raja's harem did only two or three years' service, after which they were pensioned off and presented with plots of land. These women, having property, had no trouble attracting husbands and, being of independent means, they often dominated their men after marriage, so much so that, unlike women who had never been favored by the Jat Raja, they could even be unfaithful to their husbands with impunity.

Despite Chander's revulsion at the doings of the two princelings, he felt tempted by the idea of getting to know one of the Jat Raja's pensioned-off women. But he worried about the danger not only to his moral well-being but also to his physical health. He left the hills as celibate as he had been when he arrived.

Even after Chander settled back down in Lahore, at King Edward Medical College, he could not get out of his head the vision of those beautiful young hill girls plucked and gathered like flowers and presented to the Nawab and the Jat Raja for their daily pleasure. Despite his steady moral outlook, something within him had changed. He felt agitated and unsettled.

❧

THE SUMMER AFTER his second year of medical college, Chander was drawn back to Kangra district and the hills, as if by a mysterious force. But this time he was more knowledgeable and more wary about what he could say and do. As soon as he had fallen into his routine at the dispensary, he went in search of Reshmi. He was pleasantly surprised to see that she was still there and that she was as glad to see him as he was to see her. In the intervening year, she had physically matured and acquired a healthy color in her cheeks. Through conversation with her, he gathered that she had grown more deft at deflecting her stepmother's anger and at getting her own way. He made a habit of going in the evening to the hillside where she grazed her flock. Sometimes, as she was watching the sheep they would sit on rocks in the woods by the stream, far up from the hut. They never had much to say to each other. She was poor and illiterate; he was from a good family and getting the best education available in the province. So they would mostly sit quietly, simply enjoying the feeling of being near each other.

One day, she folded her arms around her knees and her left sleeve rode up. He started. Halfway along the inside of her upper arm was tattooed, discreetly, "Meera," the name of the consort of the Hindu god Krishna.

"The tattoo is a secret," she said, quickly pulling down her sleeve. "I am going to grow up to be like Meera. I am going to marry Lord Krishna, and devote myself to him night and day."

Chander had a different impression of the devotees of Krishna than she did. He saw their worship of the god as more sensual than spiritual. Krishna was a voluptuary deity who frolicked with milkmaids, never settling down with any one of them. In fact, his devotees were notorious for cavorting with one another as lovers, with the name of Krishna on their lips. All the same, Chander was moved by the purity of Reshmi's character.

She lives on a higher spiritual plane than I do, and here I've been admiring only her physical beauty, like the wretched Nawab or the Jat Raja, he thought. Yet he desired her and spontaneously started singing a ghazal to her. His breaking out into a love song startled her and, before he could stop her, she had jumped up from her rock and run away.

Chander was sure that she would return for her sheep, but it was growing dark and he wanted to get back to the dispensary. He decided that he would not wait around for her but the next day would make his apologies and reassure her that he had meant no harm.

After work, when Chander climbed the hill to find Reshmi, however, neither she nor the sheep were in the pasture. He went to her hut, only to find the little boy sucking a mango and the woman sunning herself in the doorway.

"Where is Reshmi?" he cried.

"Reshmi didn't return last night," the woman told him in an irritated voice. "The hussy didn't even bring in the sheep— my husband had to go and fetch them."

Chander was alarmed. He wondered if he might have contributed to the girl's disappearance by scaring her with his song and making her run away into the night. Could she have fallen down a ravine? But she was a hill girl, as sure-footed as the sheep she tended. Could she have been nabbed by one of the Nawab's henchmen—wasn't that what happened to every beautiful hill girl sooner or later? It was certainly suspicious that the stepmother had made no public fuss about the girl's disappearance. Could it be that the stepmother was in cahoots with the Nawab's agents and had sold her step-daughter so that she would have more food for herself and her son to gorge themselves on?

Chander went to the police, but they had no information. He sought out the deputy commissioner, an Englishman, and reported to him the girl's disappearance.

"We don't want any meddlers like you around here," the deputy commissioner said, brushing him off.

Chander persisted, and informed the deputy commissioner that he was a student in good standing at King Edward Medical College.

"In that case, young man, I advise you to go back to Lahore and mind your books," the Englishman replied. "It's best for the plains people to leave the hill people alone with their sheep, their customs, and their religion."

Chander wanted to shout at the deputy commissioner that the British authorities were supposed to uphold law and order, but he dared not talk back to an Englishman, so he went away fuming quietly.

For the next few days, he made cautious inquiries around the hills about Reshmi; he could find no trace of her. He couldn't even locate her father, who, if the stepmother was to be believed, had left on a search mission of his own and had not come back.

Chander had a sense of foreboding. Why hadn't Reshmi's father come back, he wondered. Where could the fellow find sanctuary in the hills, where the princelings and the British authorities conspired against the people? At the first sign of trouble from him, they would find a way of silencing him. Wasn't that what the compounder had implied when he warned Chander against making any inquiries about the Nawab's nefarious activities? The princelings were sovereign in their little principalities, with the right of life and death over their subjects. It seemed that the British authorities were perfectly content to tolerate native customs, however odious, provided those customs did not threaten the British order.

Chander could do nothing but acknowledge his own helplessness and return to Lahore.

❧

CHANDER WENT BACK to the hills and to the rural dispensary for the third time. Whatever his qualms about the place, he was drawn back to the cool of the mountains, much like some birds who migrated from the plains at the onset of the summer heat. By chance, he got to know a heart specialist, a Hindu doctor with a degree from Chander's medical college, who attended the Jat Raja. Through the specialist's good offices, Chander was introduced to his employer. He was prepared to dislike the prince, but His Highness was so young, so unassuming, so natural and courteous that Chander immediately fell under his spell and conveniently put out of his mind his initial revulsion at the Prince's harem practices. Anyway, Chander was now older and, he thought, wiser and more circumspect.

The Jat Raja gave him a private tour of the palace. On the walls and floors of its reception rooms were hides of tigers, complete with claws intact and unnerving glass eyes. The Jat Raja boasted proudly that they had all been shot by his father and forefathers. As he walked Chander through the palace grounds—quite extensive for a prince of such a small hill principality, Chander thought—he pointed with even greater pride to his private clay tennis court.

"The deputy commissioner says this is one of the best tennis courts in the hills," the Jat Raja said. "That's a real compliment from an Englishman."

"Your Highness plays tennis?" Chander asked tentatively. He feared that, if the Jat Raja didn't play, his question might seem impertinent.

"Of course, young man," said the Jat Raja. "I'm not like the Nawab, who has a billiard table but no cues."

Chander did not like being addressed as "young man." He

felt he was being patronized, especially since the Jat Raja did not seem to be more than a couple of years older than he himself was. Still, mindful of the Jat Raja's exalted position, Chander did his best to be deferential.

"If you play tennis, I challenge you to a set," the Jat Raja said.

"I do, and I gladly accept."

"If you win, I'll eat a dozen mangoes, and if I win you'll eat a dozen mangoes. Are we on?"

The bet was so boorish that Chander could scarcely believe it was coming from a royal mouth. But then he remembered that the Raja came from the Jat tribe, famous for their rustic ways. In fact, when he thought about it, everything about the Jat Raja—his simple dress, his garish palace furnishings, his Jat staff—all seemed rustic.

What is extraordinary is not his bet but the fact that he plays the sophisticated Western game at all, Chander thought.

There and then, the Jat Raja shouted for a bearer to bring a couple of racquets and some balls, and the two began the match.

The Jat Raja was a good player, but Chander was better. Because Chander had heard that if you bested a prince dire things could happen, he allowed the Jat Raja to win the first game.

"You let me win because I am a raja," the Jat Raja said, grinning.

"If you say so, Your Highness," Chander said.

The next two games, Chander played to his usual standard and so handily won the set.

The Jat Raja, in an entirely unprincely way, squatted at the edge of the tennis court, called for a dozen mangoes, bit off their tops one after another, and set about sucking out the pulp. Chander, a doctor-to-be, looked on in utter astonishment—anxious about the effects that so much rich fruit could have on his opponent's digestion.

The Jat Raja was so taken with Chander that he arranged

for him to come back and stay with him as his guest for a couple of weeks, on the condition that he play a set or two of tennis with him every day.

During the stay, the Jat Raja became so free with Chander that one evening after dinner, a little like a gardener expatiating on the exotic plants in his nursery, he confided to him the number and variety of minors he had in his harem.

The old feeling of revulsion rose in Chander, but he quickly mastered it and, trying to seem like a man of the world who would have no trouble falling into step with any drumbeat, said, "Your Highness, not so long ago I myself took a fancy to a young Hindu hill girl who lived near the rural dispensary in the Nawab's state. Her name was Reshmi. Did she ever come to your notice?"

The Jat Raja wanted to know every last detail about the girl and her background. And, when he realized that none of the girls in his harem fitted the description, he became furious at the Nawab, thinking that he must have appropriated the prize Hindu hill girl for his own harem.

"I swear to you that I will not rest until I find out what happened to Reshmi," the Jat Raja said. "If the Nawab has her in his harem, I will have her spirited away from him."

Chander dismissed the oath as the bravado of an overweening prince. After he left the palace, he had no occasion to see the Jat Raja again and he did not give him or his oath much thought.

Years passed. Chander finished his medical studies in Lahore and, spurning the chance to get married and settle down, went to England for further studies.

❧

CHANDER WAS NOW an England-returned doctor. Although he was still unmarried, his student days, and his summer expeditions to the hills, had been put away like old schoolbooks. He happened to be vacationing in Simla, the summer capital of British India, so English in its character that Indians called it Chhota Vilayat (Little England), watching a tennis tournament at the Viceregal Lodge, when a man tapped him on the shoulder. He was reluctant to take his eye off the match, but when he looked around he was startled to see the Jat Raja standing there.

"Do you remember that I swore to find out what happened to that fancy of yours?"

For a moment, Chander couldn't recall what the Jat Raja was talking about.

"That young hill girl you were interested in as a student."

Chander's pulse quickened. For the first time in a long while, he remembered seeing her sleeve ride up her arm and how she had tried to hide her secret from him.

"She was not kidnapped by the Nawab at all, but by the sub-inspector of the local police," the Jat Raja said.

The pounding of the players' tennis shoes and the thwacking of their racquets hitting the ball continued as before, but Chander was oblivious of them.

"The news of the crime reached the ear of a kind Hindu gentleman, Dr. Gian Kaul, who got her away from the sub-inspector," the Jat Raja continued. "In any event, the Muslim ravager of the lower hills never laid a finger on her."

"Where is she now?" Chander asked, his mouth dry.

"Well," the Jat Raja said, with a sort of regal carelessness, "people say she was married off to a rich, ugly widower from the plains, but I doubt that he's a happy man, because people also say that his grown son partakes of her delights behind his father's back."

❧

As I worked on this chapter of my father's novel, I tried to give it appropriate atmosphere, pacing, and tone. But as it went on the material he sent me became sketchy and perfunctory, and I had trouble continuing with the story, which, in any case, often threatened to turn into a sort of Indian fairy tale. For instance, I had few details about the time that elapsed between the tennis scenes at the Jat Raja's palace and at the Viceregal Lodge, something that might be acceptable in a fairy tale but not in a serious novel. In any event, the chance meeting with the Jat Raja seemed implausible and ill prepared for, nor were the rescue and the bad marriage of the hill girl convincing. I had to gloss over and summarize those events, and that gave the narrative a hurried feel. But for all my prodding I couldn't get my father to come up with more material; it was as if he had tired of the story and wanted to wind it up anyway and anyhow. To galvanize him, I wrote him that the story could have great historical value in shedding light upon a little-known facet of the British rule in India—the odd phenomenon of six hundred and more tyrannical princes with dominion over their individual states being allowed to behave or misbehave any way they liked, so that the British monarch could be provided with a retinue of colorful vassals for ceremonial occasions. "The self-indulgence of these self-styled princelings—with harems, tiger shoots, and whatnot—is vivid stuff and worth the effort of evoking," I wrote. "Can you come up with more material about this? The venalities of these lawless potentates must have provided a great deal of amusement to the British authorities and confirmed their self-righteous view that they were not exploiters of their subjects but a superior race who were bringing the torch of civilization to a backward society." I reminded him of Kipling's verses:

Take up the White Man's burden—
    Send forth the best ye breed—
Go, bind yourselves to exile
    To serve your captives' need;
To wait in heavy harness
    On fluttered folk and wild—
Your new-caught, sullen people,
    Half devil and half child.

I could not, however, coax new material from him.

By temperament, I had difficulty leaving anything unfinished, and so I eventually wrote to my father asking, somewhat gingerly, for just enough to wind up at least the first chapter. After a long silence on the subject, he wrote back, saying that, sadly, he did not have the energy to go on, that age had caught up with him, that I should use the draft I had as a jumping-off point to write my own novel or, better still, we should forget the idea of a book altogether—instead, turn the chapter into a short story and then try to get it published as it was. He even thought that such a story might be made into a film, because he had heard that some inspired directors could work from just a few good pages of writing—he was nothing if not a dreamer. "I have many stories in my head," he wrote. "They are like the Russian dolls your sisters used to play with as children—one doll inside another. How I wish I were twenty, thirty years younger, so that I could unpack them and lay them all out for you."

My father's abandoning the project in midstream put me in a quandary. The chapter had been cast as an introduction to a novel on a big scale, with a big canvas in mind, and there was no way of condensing it into a short story. Yet I couldn't badger him to go on with the book, nor could I go on with it on my own. The period and its goings on were outside the range of my experience, my knowledge, and almost my imagination. But I felt there was no point in telling any of this to him and ruffling his old age.

Long after I had concluded that nothing could be done with the novel, he sent me not one but three possible endings for the chapter. In one ending, Reshmi's husband died, and she settled in the hills as a middle-aged recluse, guarded by two large ferocious dogs and living with her strapping, ugly stepson as his dutiful mistress. In the second ending, Chander got married and sired a family of his own, after which he and Reshmi became lovers. He treated her as a second, illicit wife, only to break off with her when he came to realize that the scandal would damage the chances of his arranging good marriages for his daughters. In the third and longest ending, Chander and Reshmi lost contact for decades, but he never stopped dreaming of her and searching for her. He finally found her as an elderly holy woman, living in a lonely cottage in the upper hills near the palace of the Jat Raja. During their momentous meeting, she quietly got up, brought out a sitar from a corner of the cottage, sat down on the floor with the instrument, fastidiously arranged and rearranged under her the white sari she was wearing, tuned the sitar, and played a raga that stirred him to distraction. After that, they sat in silence for a little while. Then she gently but firmly showed him the door, and asked him never to come back. He went down the hill like an Indian Orpheus, under an injunction never to look back—and he never did.

The endings were all unsatisfactory, like the hiatus between the two tennis scenes. In one, Chander didn't even appear. In any event, the scenes jumped ahead thirty or forty years without giving any idea of what might have happened in the interim. I felt I had no choice but to abandon the project once and for all. Then, slowly but surely, some new material came my way, and this material was so unexpected and riveting that I felt the need to continue with the story on my own, a story no doubt different from the one my father had originally intended to write but, nonetheless, inextricably related to it.

II

WOVEN INTO THE

REGION

I N THE SUMMER OF 1974, I WAS IN NEW DELHI DOING research for a book about Mahatma Gandhi. I needed a certain amount of privacy and independence to read and write, and to see people for my work. Thus, I was staying not with my parents, in their cramped little house, but at the India International Centre, a sort of club-cum-hostel for Indian scholars and visiting foreigners. A room and meals there cost much less than what they cost at a Western-type hotel. For the Gandhi book, I would travel through the hinterlands, trudging through villages and into hovels, eating anywhere and whatever, but then gladly retreat to the Centre, with its modern conveniences of running hot water and flush toilets and its good food, feeling guilty, however, as if I were turning the clock back to pre-Independence, undemocratic days, when government servants and army officers lived in their specially created islands of civil lines and military cantonments, all set apart from the people and the rest of the country.

The Centre had been built with government subsidies, and it had open lawns, was thick with all manner of flowering bushes, and served Westernized Indian, or Indianized Western, food—which came to the same thing. But at the time its accommodations resembled those of a cheap American motel. The rooms had flimsy walls, platform beds with foam-rubber mattresses, and wicker chairs. Although ground-floor rooms were equipped with elegant French doors, so that guests could step out onto the lawn, say, or enjoy the monsoon breezes, everyone kept them tightly shut against insects and city detritus. Both the rooms and the halls had a pervasive, noxious smell of pesticides, which were liberally applied to every corner of the place to kill the cockroaches and the like—themselves reminders of the pestilence that was always threatening to invade every outpost of Western modernity in impoverished India.

My father had his own club, the Gymkhana, where he went in the evening. Designed in the British period for the English and a few select Indian officials, and replete with tennis courts, clubhouses, and manicured verdant grounds, it had been brought into being almost in defiance of the general Indian disorder of crowds, slums, and bazaars, and had once had an aura of great splendor and well-being. But lately, like other foreign transplants in independent India, the facilities had fallen into disrepair and acquired a shabby, nearly greasy aspect. Still, my father was proud of his membership in the club and had gone to the lengths of making all of us children members, as if membership in it were a privilege that had to be husbanded and passed on like a legacy. Indeed, for every one member now elected there were thousands waiting to get in. That was the fate of all modern Indian institutions, because of the galloping rise of the population. My father had adapted to the changes in the club, as to those in the country at large. But whenever I went there I came away feeling depressed. I remember swimming in the pool and being driven out by its chlorination, no doubt overly concentrated to compensate for the poor condition of the filtering system. When I mentioned my experience to my father, he said, "People like you, who live in the West, get used to a whole different standard of things, but we have to make the best of things as they are here." Like most Indian houses, his house had no running hot water, and he looked forward to going to his club in the evenings for a hot shower, just as, after travelling, I looked forward to getting back to the India International Centre. We used to laugh that, when we were in our separate clubs, we were both temporarily cut off from the "real India."

❧

ONE EVENING, MY FATHER stopped by my room at the Centre on his way to the Gymkhana. He was carrying with him an old, battered leather attaché case with two latch locks, in which he usually carried his change of clothes to and from the club. I was amused that a man of my father's age and stature still carried the same kind of attaché case that we children had used to carry our change of clothes in when we were travelling on trains. In those days, within the first half hour of our travel our clothes, along with our faces, hands, and knees, would be coated with gritty soot flying through the open windows from the anthracite coal that fired the engine, and before reaching our destination we would have to change. I now tried to relieve my father of the attaché case, but he hugged it as if it were a precious object, laying it next to his chair as he sat down. He made himself comfortable, though, by taking off his shoes and putting his feet up on the bed.

"Do you remember the endings to 'Hill Girls' that I sent you?" he asked abruptly, but in a casual voice. "I've been thinking that we should continue the story."

I hadn't thought about the story since we abandoned it some years earlier. It had languished in a drawer with my other manuscripts that, for one reason or another, hadn't worked out.

"Gosh, that comes as a surprise," I said to my father. "I thought you had no more material."

"Well, I was thinking that we could leap ahead to a time when Reshmi is a beautiful grown woman and Chander is a married man. He could run into her, and they could end up having a love affair—becoming bewitched with each other, so to speak. Their love affair would last for two heavenly years, during which they would live more or less like Europeans. We could call that their Enchanted Period."

"'Live like Europeans'—what would that mean? Remember, Reshmi was a simple shepherdess from the hills."

"That's true. But when I was young George Bernard Shaw was all the rage with us students, and I remember reading his 'Pygmalion.' Well, let the hill girl be the Indian version of Eliza Doolittle. After all, Shaw's heroine was just a simple flower peddler until she was taken up by Professor Higgins. G.B.S. made her transformation into a lady extremely convincing."

The idea seemed outlandish, but I wanted to draw my father out. Talking to him about the story seemed so much easier than corresponding with him about it. I even felt a little excitement at the thought of picking up the old draft.

"What kind of person would the hill girl become?" I asked. "How would she and Chander meet again? And wouldn't it be better if Chander was a bachelor? The story thus far is written on simple lines, almost like a fairy tale, and I think it would be best to keep to that tone."

"I haven't thought about many of the details yet. All I can envision so far is a love affair between Reshmi and Chander, just like what people have in the West, with sex, as you would call it today. During the Raj, such love affairs occurred among, perhaps, the British, but not among members of good Indian families like Chander's."

"But how would we explain Chander's suddenly acting like a European? So far in the story, we have him as an innocent medical student, if England-returned. To make a shift in his character like the one you propose would require a lot of work. We'd have to develop his character, which would take pages and pages. And if you did have him having an affair, wouldn't he have to deal with terrible scandals and consequences? Then, if in addition you have him married, how would we deal with the problem of his spouse? Remember, Reshmi is already married in the story, so we'll have the problem of dealing not with one spouse but two. That will really make for a complicated melodrama, maybe a soap opera, which wouldn't work alongside the pastoral story that we have so far."

"I think that could be handled by their exchanging a lot of Red Letters."

"What do you mean by 'Red Letters'?"

"I mean love letters. Red, as you know, is the color of love and of danger—it would be a tip-off to the reader of what we're up to. In fact, we could tell much of the story of the romance through the Red Letters. The letters could be intimate. Near the end of the story, Reshmi would beg Chander to burn them, but he wouldn't be able to do it, because they would be so dear to his heart. Yet he would be afraid that, if they fell into anyone's hands, they would ruin the chances of his daughters' ever getting married. So, instead of burning them he would seal them in an envelope and would secretly entrust them to a close relative with the injunction that he should return them whenever Chander asks for them or else burn them in the event of Chander's death. Many years later, Chander would retrieve the letters, reread them, and relive the Enchanted Period."

"Stories told through letters, however intimate, tend to be dull. Nowadays, writers avoid the epistolary form for a novel, if that's what you have in mind. It lacks the force and immediacy of, say, a first-person narrative."

"I think that if those Red Letters were written properly, you might think differently. You might find them to be so singular and beautiful that they could be a story in themselves."

"It sounds as if you have already started writing them. If I could read your draft, I could tell you what I think of them."

"I wish, son, I had the imagination to compose such letters, but I am no more capable of that than I am of re-creating the enchantment of the Raj in all its glory."

My father had talked on for so long that the time for his going to the club for his hot shower had passed. He decided to take a shower and change at the Centre instead, so that he could be home in time to have dinner with my mother.

❦

MY FATHER AGAIN stopped by my room at the Centre in the evening on the way to his club. As on the earlier visit, he would not let me take the attaché case from him and sat down with it next to him. He put his feet up on the bed and started talking as if we had never left off. "I've been thinking more about our story," he began. "Chander's wife, whom I will call Shakuntala, and Reshmi will become such good friends that they will be almost like sisters. Reshmi will be so beautiful, outside and inside, that everyone will fall in love with her. Even after Shakuntala comes to know about the love affair, she will overlook it, and that will raise her in Chander's estimation. Then Shakuntala will refer to Reshmi not with malice but with sympathy. This will endear Shakuntala to Chander all the more."

I again emphasized to him that we should try to keep the story simple, that otherwise it would get out of hand, and that there was all the difference between just talking about things like Chander and Reshmi's having an affair and making those things plausible on paper. But he was in no mood to be reined in. It seemed that he had been plotting the story in his head and was fired up with ideas. Since I had originally been thwarted by lack of material in my attempt to continue the story, I thought that it was best for me now not to check him in his rediscovered enthusiasm. Maybe his new material could stir the embers and reignite the fire under the project.

"Since Shakuntala will know about the affair, a reader would expect her to scratch Reshmi's eyes out," I said, falling in step with his mood.

"But, I tell you, their relationship will be as unique as Reshmi's relationship with Chander. In fact, at the most intense time of the Enchanted Period Shakuntala and Reshmi together will knit a red sweater for Chander. Shakuntala will work on the back and Reshmi on the front, and they will race to see who can knit faster. Shakuntala will be a faster knitter, but Reshmi will win in her own way: she will surreptitiously weave a lock of her hair into the region of the heart. That red sweater will last longer than any other sweater Chander owns. It will be lost, but not because of Shakuntala's unconscious resentment that Reshmi had a hand in it, as you might think, but because of some political upheaval, like perhaps the Partition."

"Would Shakuntala know about the lock of Reshmi's hair?"

"Yes. She will eventually find out everything. She will have her own shrewd ways, picked up in the corrupting *gullis* of the city, which will be unknown to Chander, who will have grown up in the innocent lanes of his village."

I had to do a kind of mental somersault. The way he was portraying Chander's and Shakuntala's backgrounds was eerily reminiscent of the way he had always contrasted my mother's upbringing in the city with his own in a village. Indeed, all along I had been aware that there were more than passing resemblances between him and Chander, such as that both had been students at King Edward Medical College, that both were "England-returned," and that both had been guests at the Viceregal Lodge in Simla. While working on the draft of "Hill Girls," I'd assumed that he was using these real settings because, not being a writer, he had trouble coming up with verisimilitudes. I felt I should not tamper with his settings in case it stopped his flow. They could easily be taken care of at a later stage of writing. I now began to wonder, however, whether Chander and Shakuntala were thin disguises for people in his own life—even actually modelled after him and my mother themselves. Could it be that what all along he had presented to me as fictional material had a basis in fact? In a way, that would not be surprising, since he was essentially a government official and it would be more difficult for him to invent people and events than to write from his real experience. If my hunch was right, then who was Reshmi? I couldn't puzzle it out. I now asked him what in law is called a leading question: "What will Reshmi end up doing?"

"She will give herself over to religion, as in one of the old story endings that you didn't like. She is in her late sixties and is thinking about freeing herself from worldly passions. She constantly recites verses from the Bhagvat Gita. Some change was to be expected, since forty years have passed since the Enchanted Period."

Certainly, his having slipped from conditional into indicative mood, and then from future into present tense, all but confirmed my surmise. The mention of the exact figure of forty years also set off certain bells in my head, as if I were approaching some kind of denouement in my understanding, a moment when the disguises might fall away, as at the end of a play, when actors take a curtain call and reveal themselves to be ordinary people. But I was mindful of the explosive nature of the material. "Sex, as you would call it today." I had to approach him gingerly, not only for his sake but also for mine—for in the balance were my lifelong glowing notions of his rectitude and of the purity and stability of his forty-nine-year-long marriage to my mother.

"Forty years?" I put my question tentatively, so as not to disturb him—disturb the trancelike atmosphere of our conversation.

"Yes, forty years, almost on the button. In that span of time, it might be natural for a person like Reshmi to change so radically as to be able to forget her time with Chander. But Chander cannot forget the dalliance. Fortunately or unfortunately, he has a good memory. The moment he remembers something, the whole scene appears vividly in front of his eyes, as if it were taking place right now, rather than in some distant past."

Even as I was being brought perilously close to the idea that the story might actually be about him, I felt there was no way I could handle the thought of my father in an extramarital relationship. Could it be that he had based Shakuntala and Chander on my mother and himself and brought in the love affair with Reshmi only because he thought that a story based on a love triangle would make for much more dramatic fiction than one based on a happy marriage? After all, he had planned to write a spicy story that might wow a film producer. I was trying my best to avoid admitting a certainty that was now on the edge of my consciousness.

He settled back the way he used to when we were children and he had come back from an especially taxing tour of inspection and wanted to take a catnap before going to his club for tennis, bridge, or poker. He went on now, almost as if he were talking to himself, in a dreamy tone, as if he were not even aware that he was speaking. I felt like an eavesdropper. "Ah, that Enchanted Period. To Chander, a lock of golden hair, enclosed in one of Reshmi's letters, will forever remain hallowed. How he will remember her lovely hair, so long and thick that someone could get lost in it and so light that she could have passed for a European. Oh, son," he said, as if suddenly becoming aware of my presence, "I cannot describe to you what memories are revived in Chander by that lock of hair and what palpitations they cause. Words entirely fail, and fail miserably. A chance meeting with Reshmi in his old age evoked such warm feelings for her in Chander that he himself was surprised. He is in the evening of his life and feels that all that was is worthwhile. I am reminded of an Urdu couplet: 'Let the light of your memories abide with me. / I know not in what lane my old age shall pass.'"

A bit like haiku in Japan, Urdu couplets were a celebrated,

pithy verse form in India. They encapsulated the wisdom of the ages and the lessons of life. People who could neither read nor write instinctively turned to them for solace and enlightenment, as indeed my father himself had, for as long as I could remember. In his case, though, they were more than that. Having been schooled in the old court tradition of speaking and writing Persian and Urdu and learning by rote, he seemed to have an inexhaustible store of Urdu couplets and was never at a loss for an apt one for any occasion or situation. They would come to his lips unbidden and cap and memorialize the moment.

It was impossible for me to go on believing that the character of Chander was not based on my father. I was stunned by the insight, even as I realized that, in some part of my mind, I must have sensed the truth all along and been afraid to follow the obvious clues to unsettling conclusions.

Perhaps he has been using the subterfuge of the novel only to dull the pain of his confession, I thought. As my mother had always said, "Your daddy can't keep anything in his belly. He wears his heart on his sleeve."

Gradually, he confided that "Hill Girls" was true in its main outline—that Chander was Amolak Ram, that is to say himself, that Shakuntala was Shanti, my mother, and that Reshmi was my mother's close friend, whom we had called Auntie Rasil since childhood.

His confidence was jarring, and it made me acutely sensitive to every little sound around me, the way I used to be when I was running a high fever as a child. At those times, the clink of a spoon against my mother's teacup and the scrape of my father's razor on his cheek, the click-click of my mother's knitting needles and the tick-tick of my father's wristwatch would be amplified, as if they were not outside but inside my head. Now, in the India International Centre—through whose thin walls I was always subliminally aware of people talking and hacking in their rooms and bathrooms—my fevered brain was assaulted by the sound of some American anthropologists down the hall having a noisy discussion about Indian customs. I wanted to go out and tell them to shut up or, alternatively, ask them to come into my room and learn something from my father. But I felt paralyzed, fixed to my wicker chair.

I fastened on one of many objections that came rushing into my head. "Surely, you must have been a medical student just after the war. At that time, a little hill princeling could not have had a motorcar, never mind with curtains and whatnot."

He laughed, relieving the tension. "All writers use *mirch* and masala here and there—spice things up for the reader."

❦

RASIL'S IDENTITY, LIKE that of everyone else who might be embarrassed by what follows, has been disguised; in any case, Rasil is no longer alive. The account of my parents, however, is as truthful as I can make it, and I am able to write it now only because my father has been dead since 1986 and my mother since 1990. Moreover, before my father died he gave me his express permission to write about this, in my own way, but only when sufficient time had passed to avoid hurting or distressing anyone involved. He left the judgment of when that might be to me. Since his original revelation, more than a quarter of a century has elapsed. During that time I did not so much as say a word about it. I did not even glance at my notes of our conversations. But since then, because of the spread of television, satellite dishes, and travel and the advent of e-mail and cell phones—the dissemination of Western ideas, generally—Indian customs and moral codes have been undergoing a drastic change. Indeed, my father's India has been overtaken. Much of his clan has experienced a diaspora, with family members now settled in places as far away as Australia and Canada. Many of my parents' eighteen grandchildren are married and have children of their own. It is because of such changes, too, that I can now think of publishing the secret. In fact, with the passage of time my parents' lives have acquired the sanctity of history, and the secret has lost all but historical interest. Whether or what I write about them is a matter mainly for my conscience.

Even so, I write what follows with considerable trepidation. Originally, when my father confided in me, he put his trust in my word, and, no matter how I justify and rationalize it, I can't help but wonder if I am being self-serving or vengeful by using his most private memories as material for my writing. Anyway, by the nature of my vocation I am ill-suited to keep secrets. In writing a series of books about myself and my family, among other things, with the title Continents of Exile, I have often been torn between loyalty to my family and loyalty to my craft, to which any kind of censorship is anathema. My father, who served as a source for some of the material, knew all too well how such conflicts tormented me. He also knew that I was always able to negotiate my way between the feelings of the people I was writing about and the demands of my craft—by disguising people and places, among other stratagems. In any event, he, like me, sensed, even as he was confiding in me, that the story had a larger significance, something neither of us could yet verbalize, but which we imagined would far transcend his life—and maybe mine, too.

❧

"THE LOVE AFFAIR had ended before you were born," my father said, as if he sensed my agitation and wanted to reassure me.

"But I remember Auntie Rasil. I think she used to come to our house in Simla. But I have trouble believing that the Reshmi we wrote about in 'Hill Girls' could be the same person as Rasil. We portrayed the character as a rustic shepherdess, but the woman I remember was a sophisticated socialite."

"They were one and the same, son. That was her magic, the romance of her. As a girl, she was exactly the way I described Reshmi, and as a woman she was exactly the way you would remember Auntie Rasil."

Now that I thought about it, when I was growing up I had heard about a real twelve-year-old hill girl whom my father had treated when he was a medical student. I had even written about her in passing in "Daddyji," two years before, but so strong was my wish to deny that that girl could have had anything to do with the fictional Reshmi—the girl sitting with Chander on the rock or the woman knitting the lock of hair into his sweater—that, despite an abundance of telltale signs, it hadn't struck me until this evening that Reshmi was a real person throughout. I can only explain my obtuseness by the fact that, as a good son, I wanted to deny not only that my father might have had an illicit relationship during his marriage but also that he had ever been interested in any other woman besides my mother. All the same, I now asked myself, "How could I have been so naïve? How did I not catch on to the relationship with Rasil when I was doing research for 'Daddyji'?" Although the facts in the book had not changed, the realization that certain critical facts were absent was already causing me to shift my perspective on the book and the life as described in it. I immediately chastised myself for thinking about myself—my book, my perspective—when I should have been thinking about my mother: what she must have gone through, what she must have suffered.

I tried to recall everything I had felt as a child about Rasil in order to conjure her up. I was probably the only one in the family who never took to her, and I think that that had to do with her harsh, nasal, almost grating voice.

"I don't think I liked her," I now said to my father. "Her voice put me off. In my experience, there is always a correlation between voice and character—I would have said voice and looks, except that I know people said she was one of the most beautiful women in the Punjab."

"Her voice might have been a vestige of the poor hill girl she had once been that survived her transformation into a well-to-do Punjabin," my father said. "But that was her only imperfection, and I thought it only succeeded in setting off her dazzling beauty. Anyway, I doubt that you remember her voice from Simla. You were just three when we left there, in 1937. You must be remembering her voice from later meetings, in Lahore."

"I don't know where I remember her from, exactly, but I do remember that she had the voice of the witch on a children's radio program I used to listen to as a child. I remember distinctly once saying to Mamaji that Auntie Rasil sounded like the radio witch, and she said, 'Go put a coal on your tongue. If you could see her, you would take her for a queen.' I wasn't so sure. I continued to imagine her as half witch, half fairy."

"She must have made a great impression on you if you still remember what you thought of her as child," my father said.

"How could she not? Somehow, I must have got the sense that she was someone important to you and Mamaji. Now I wonder if she'd bewitched both of you, in different ways."

"Well, well, well, son. You would have to know much more than you do now to reach such a conclusion, and anyway I'm not sure that such a judgment would be fair to your dear mother, Rasil, or me."

I felt I had been hasty and had overstepped the bounds of propriety. I had no right to make judgments like that, and he was right to reproach me. In any case, I worried that I was being curious for the sake of being curious, instead of thinking about the consequences of such a powerful revelation. I said tentatively, "Of course, I would like to know more, but it's really up to you what you would like to tell or keep back."

"Yes, yes," he said abstractedly, as if he were also of two minds about how far he should go in confiding in me, perhaps for fear of the effects on both him and me. He went on thoughtfully, "Remember, son, because you have guessed, I cannot keep back from you the truth, but whatever confidences I make to you are only for your ears. They are to be locked up in your heart, never revealed to your mother or anyone else."

"Is that injunction permanent?"

"It is"—and he paused—"until I release you from it. Or, at least, until your dear mother and I are no longer alive."

I couldn't imagine ever divulging to anyone things in his life that he wished to keep private. Ever since I was a child, people had always trusted me with their secrets, as if because I was blind I were incapable of betraying them, and over the years keeping secrets had become second nature to me. I felt, however, that for my own enlightenment I had to clear up one point about my father's secret: If it was so sacrosanct, why had he risked portraying his romance in a novel? He could not have been unaware that some people would be able to see through the disguises, even if they hadn't been as transparent as they actually were. I asked him about this now.

Rather than answering my question directly, he simply said, "Maybe one day you'll have to pick up the threads of the novel and go on with it. As I told you, my imagination is not up to the task—it's no longer as supple as it used to be. I wish I had started writing the novel when I was young and was brimming over with energy. Now all I can say to myself in the way of solace about the Enchanted Period is said in an Urdu couplet: 'Spent a few moments of utter happiness. / The remembrance of those is my life.'"

After my father had gone that evening, the more I thought about his revelation, the more staggering it seemed. I was already older than he had been during the Enchanted Period, but thinking of him swanning about with Rasil in Simla, perhaps exchanging billets-doux with her, as people did in Europe, was troubling. Should he, as my father, have been telling any of this to me? Was it right for me, as his son, to be receiving his confidences in such an intimate matter? Had I unwittingly coaxed the confession from him? Once I had stumbled upon the truth, should I have deflected him from further confidences? But had I even had that choice? Certainly, when we started out on his novel neither he nor I could have foreseen how far and deep it would take us into the dark corners of his personal history. Since he was not a professional writer, and so not trained in devising verisimilitude, his characterizations had turned out to be transparent, and so he was put in the impossible position of having to deny what I had guessed to be true. If I encouraged him to talk on, it was only because he seemed to enjoy revisiting the memory of the Enchanted Period, as if he had kept it buried inside him for so long that it was a relief for him to bring it finally into the open. It was too much to expect him to disown a past that he cherished. At his age, the stolen kisses in memory might even seem more enticing than they had been in the Simla hills almost half a century earlier. Seen from this perspective, the fact that his confidant happened to be his son was circumstantial and irrelevant. In any case, the whole sequence of events had been set into motion because I was a writer, and as a writer I was trying to embrace the truth, instead of being squeamish and judgmental. In a way, I already felt a sense of relief in saying goodbye to the artifices of Chander and Reshmi and beginning to think of the two of them as my father and Rasil.

Yet I was as sure as I could be that he had never consciously meant to divulge his secret to anyone. Traditionally, Hindus went to the cremation ground with their family secrets. Nothing was more important than to keep the reputation of the family pure and unbesmirched. Certainly my mother would have died before breathing a word of any such thing to anyone. Now that it had been vouchsafed to me, I had to keep in mind that my father was the head of the Mehta clan and occupied an exalted position and that the secret had the power to cast a shadow on his grandchildren, his cousins, his nieces, and his nephews and, perhaps, on his memory. Then, how was one to explain his having begun to write the fictional account in the first place? I fancied that all along there indeed had been something of the writer in him and that, in getting me to collaborate with him on "Hill Girls," he had seen a chance to give an artistic form to his memories. As he said, if he had embarked on the project when he was young he and I together might have been able to bring off the novel he wanted without anyone else in the world suspecting that at the heart was a true story. Certainly my mother and Rasil would never have read it, my mother because she had only a rudimentary knowledge of English and had difficulty reading any of the books that I wrote, and Rasil because she had long since become oblivious of the goings on in our family.

However I rationalized the confidences of my father, there was no question that they had already changed the way I thought about my parents' marriage. In some part of my mind, I had always idealized it. The fact that as people they were so different and yet had adapted to each other only made it seem more solid and more remarkable. They had brought us up to believe in the virtues of arranged marriage, saying that it was the best structure for nurturing love and family. As a traditional woman, my mother had sacrificed any of her own aspirations for my father and for us children, and so had bonded my father to her. He, in his turn, had done everything he could for her and for us children. In their different ways, they had both made enormous sacrifices to give every last one of us seven children the best available education. By our all living through and for one another, I fancied, their love and marriage, together with our family, had grown like a flowering tree. All of their children except me were now married and had children of their own and were sacrificing and forbearing in their own ways. I was an aberration for various reasons, some ascertainable and others not. All the same, I still hoped to emulate my parents' example and bring up a family. But now I had somehow to accommodate, in my view of my parents' marriage, the idea of my father's having had a dalliance—"mistress" was still not a word I could countenance in connection with him. Of course, at one level I understood that people sometimes had extramarital affairs—in a country like France it was almost obligatory. But, like a child, I had continued to hold my parents to a different standard. Now all the props of marriage and family that I had put my faith in seemed to collapse at once. In fact, the revelation that my father had had feet of clay seemed to augur for me a life of loneliness: I could no longer believe that anything out there in the world, even marriage, could mitigate my feeling of being alone. My despair was not long-lasting (I knew rationally that my life was separate from his, after all), but it was no less intense for that.

❦

My father continued to stop at the Centre and take his hot showers there instead of at his club. In the course of his visits, the subject of Rasil would inevitably come up at one time or another, as if the boat, once launched, could not be called back. Given my tidy temperament, I of course wanted to sort out exactly what was fiction and what was fact in "Hill Girls." But I had decided to renounce that interest until it had become clear to me that he was determined to keep nothing back. Soon, however, it was as though he thought that if he made a clean breast of all the details to me, that would stave off any critical judgment on my part—even as though he wanted to justify his conduct to me, his erstwhile biographer.

"Except for the names and those endings I dreamt up because you wanted me to, everything in 'Hill Girls' is true," he volunteered early on.

"You knew the compounder and the stepmother? There was a real Nawab and a real Jat Raja, with their own individual harems? And you really did meet the Jat Raja again at the Viceregal Lodge?"

"Yes. I needn't remind you that, as a medical man, I found it easier to write the truth than to invent."

"Do you know anything more about Rasil's past than what we wrote in 'Hill Girls'?"

"In all the time I knew Rasil, she was always tight-lipped about her past and would respond to any questions about it with a Mona Lisa smile. But I think her natural mother probably came from the Gaddis tribe in Nepal. That tribe is famous for the fair complexion of its people and the great beauty of its women."

"Reshmi in 'Hill Girls' seemed so poor and ill-educated, but Auntie Rasil spoke good English, with a charming accent."

"She was a thin, poor, illiterate girl when I first met her at the rural dispensary in Kangra district, just as we described her," he said. "But after her abduction she was rescued by a pair of philanthropists, father and son, who had an enlightened attitude toward rape victims. Like me, they were followers of Arya Samaj"—the Hindu reform movement—"and as such were dedicated to ridding Hinduism of superstition through education. They took the girl in—she was thirteen then—and saw to it that she grew up to be an accomplished lady, though she was never able to speak either Hindi or English without a Nepalese accent."

"Where did you first come across her? Outside Kangra, I mean."

"That's a long story."

❦

AS MY FATHER told it, in 1929, four years after his marriage to my mother, he was posted in Lahore as a public-health officer. One night, when he had just changed into his pyjamas and was getting ready for bed, a servant came running to say that he was wanted on the telephone.

"At this late hour? Who could it be?" my mother asked.

My father hurried to the telephone in the drawing room.

"I need you urgently, Doctor Sahib," a wheedling voice on the telephone said.

It took my father a couple of seconds to recognize the man on the telephone as Fatumal, a rich businessman who had inveigled the title of Rai Sahib from the government. In the hierarchy of British honors, it was a low-level title awarded only to "natives," but it gave people who had it a certain social cachet. My father had recently met Fatumal at the Cosmopolitan Club, the center of Lahore Indian society, and although he generally liked and accepted everyone, he had experienced an aversion to him on sight. Fatumal, for his part, no doubt impressed by my father's great popularity at the club and by his grand manner, had latched on to him, perhaps seeing in him a possible patron and protector.

"What can I do for you, Rai Sahib?" my father said on the telephone, a bit stiffly, holding the receiver away from his ear as if the fellow's voice were distasteful to him.

"I beg you—I touch your feet, Doctor Sahib," Fatumal whined. "It's a medical emergency. You can't refuse me."

It is just like him to adopt a subservient manner when the appropriate thing in an emergency would be to appeal to me as a professional man in a straightforward way, my father thought.

"You know I am a public-health officer and am not accustomed to treating private patients," my father said. "You should call your own doctor."

"No, no, Doctor Sahib, it must be you," Fatumal said. "You see, it's my wife."

It was a subject of gossip at the club how Fatumal, an ugly widower, had got himself a dazzling wife who was hardly older than his own teen-age son. That Fatumal sounded so distraught and that it was a woman in trouble seemed to leave my father no choice. "I'll be right over," he said directly.

In a few quick movements he put down the telephone, ran to the bedroom, pulled on his shirt and trousers, and picked up a stethoscope and a blood-pressure instrument that he kept at home, in case one of the children got sick—by now, he had two daughters and a third child on the way. Soon he was rushing along in his Model A Ford to Fatumal's bungalow on the other side of Lawrence Gardens. As he approached it, he was struck by its size and its imposing aspect.

The night watchman, a fierce-looking Pathan with a big stick, opened the gate, and Fatumal was waiting on the front veranda not with an anxious, panicky expression, as my father had expected, but with a conspiratorial grin.

"What's wrong with your wife, Rai Sahib—will you take me to her?" my father asked.

"Let us sit down and talk things over calmly," Fatumal said.

"It's past midnight," my father said querulously. "My wife is sitting up for me at home. Is there an emergency or not?"

"I need to talk to you about my marriage, Doctor Sahib."

My father sat down, so angry at being called out at such an hour for no medical reason he could determine that he felt like slapping Fatumal across the face—a ratlike face, with a narrow forehead, beady black eyes, and a crooked nose.

"Please do come to the point, Rai Sahib."

"You see, Doctor Sahib, I came home a little while ago—" Fatumal broke off.

"Yes?"

"Well, my wife, you know. Well, what can I say? She was carrying on with my son Ravinder. I saw this with my own two eyes. I ordered Ravinder out, but she fell to the floor, senseless. You see now why I could not call our own doctor. It must all be kept private."

"Where is she—can I examine her?"

Fatumal stood up and reluctantly led the way into his bedroom, where a dishevelled woman lay unconscious on the floor, her long fair hair loose and falling every which way. A big gray Alsatian dog stood by her head and growled at my father as he bent down to examine her.

Fatumal gave the dog a vigorous kick and it scampered to the other side of the room, yelping.

My father called for water and pinched the woman's nose. She opened her eyes, slowly came to, and sat up. Something about her face struck him, though he couldn't have said what it was. He busied himself studying the black-and-blue marks on her face and forearms.

"Where did you get all these bruises?" he asked.

"It's nothing," she said, trying to pull away.

My father glanced up at Fatumal severely, but Fatumal merely stood over her, looking concerned.

My father pushed up the woman's sleeve, to see how far up her arm she was bruised. She struggled with him, but, before he let go of her, he noticed that halfway along the inside of her upper arm was tattooed, discreetly, "Meera." The shock of recognition was overwhelming.

"God Almighty!" he all but blurted out.

❦

IN 1920, NINE years before my father saw Rasil's tattoo for the second time, he was preparing to go to England for his post-graduate medical training. He called on Dr. Gian Kaul, an England-returned family friend, to get some tips about life in England. Much to his surprise, Dr. Kaul tried to persuade him to give up thoughts of England and instead get married to a beautiful girl of seventeen whom he and his father, Munmohan Kaul, who had the British title for Indians of Rai Bahadur, were bringing up as their ward. My father told him right off the bat that he didn't want to marry anybody—that he was a restless bird and not ready to build a nest. In fact, he was so eager to get out and see the world that he didn't even ask who the girl was. (Until he returned from England and met the Jat Raja at the tennis court at the Viceregal Lodge, he did not know that Rasil was the girl Dr. Kaul had proposed for him—or, indeed, that the Kauls were the philanthropists who had rescued her from the clutches of the police sub-inspector.) After my father rebuffed Dr. Kaul's offer, Dr. Kaul was approached by Fatumal, who had heard about Rasil's beauty and was champing at the bit to marry her. Fatumal was in the market for a decorative wife who could also be a stepmother to his two sons—one a teen-ager somewhat younger than Rasil, and the other a small boy. The good doctor initially resisted the proposal from Fatumal, who was more than twice Rasil's age, was short, with a potbelly, and was black as pitch with kinky hair. Still, ultimately he capitulated and gave Rasil to him in marriage.

"If Dr. Kaul took such a dislike to Fatumal, why did he do that?" I asked. "Surely other suitors would have come along in time."

"Dr. Kaul more than disliked Fatumal," my father said. "He perceived him to be a cunning weasel of a man. But, after her rape and forcible possession by the police sub-inspector, Rasil was an outcast everywhere. On top of it, she was a penniless girl without a family at her back. Dr. Kaul must have tried his level best to conceal her unsavory past, but Fatumal, being a wily fellow, must have guessed at the truth and seen his opportunity. Anyway, Fatumal was rich: he had made a lot of money as a contractor for the railways. And, despite everything, Dr. Kaul would have seen Fatumal as acting honorably, because he pledged several good deeds if Rasil was given to him in marriage. He promised to make a big donation to the Arya Samaj, a cause which, as I told you, was close to the good doctor's heart. He also promised to adopt Shoni, Rasil's half sister, who had been born since Rasil's abduction and was one or two years old at the time of Fatumal's proposal. By then, Rasil's father had given up his sheep and was working as a night watchman in the hill station of Dalhousie, not far from his home in Kangra."

"But the fact seems to be that it suited Dr. Kaul to get rid of beautiful Auntie Rasil by marrying her off to a man who you say looked like an ogre."

"In our society, people generally don't pay any attention to the way a man looks, provided he has a good job or money— they only care how the girl looks. For Dr. Kaul, the most important consideration, therefore, would have been the kind of home Fatumal would provide for Rasil. I cannot emphasize enough the importance of Rasil's history—that, through no fault of her own, she was not a virgin and therefore could not be married off in an ordinary way. Hindu girls know that Hindu men always want virgin brides, so they always keep the example of chaste Sita before their eyes. As you know, to this day the bridegroom's relatives will spread a white sheet on the bridal bed and come in the morning after the wedding to inspect it. If they don't find blood on the sheet, the bride is packed off back to her family in disgrace—in extreme cases, the bride is even murdered. Dr. Kaul must have been mindful of this issue. Anyway, even the parents of a virgin who was from a high caste and a good family might not have been able to resist an offer from a rich widower like Fatumal."

"If Fatumal was as cunning as you say, why would he have taken her?"

"He was getting perhaps the most beautiful girl in our province as an ornament, a slave, a toy. She had a mountain complexion and European looks and had already put her tribal ways behind her and mastered the English tongue as well as the manners of our women who went to convent schools and colleges. On top of it, she had natural elegance and refined ways. Somehow or other, word of her phenomenal beauty and accomplishments had spread far and wide."

I had assumed that social position could not be purchased in the caste-conscious, hidebound India of those days. Moreover, in the India I knew stains on one's reputation, whether they were of one's own making or not, could never be wiped clean. It was therefore hard for me to understand how Rasil, who by background and history was a social outcast, could have gone on to become a socially prominent person. "I would have thought that word of Auntie Rasil's past would have dogged her all her life," I said. "How was the transformation from the hill girl you knew to the Auntie Rasil I knew accomplished?"

"With Rai Sahib's money and her beauty," my father said, "those people who knew about her past made it a point either to overlook or to forget it."

❧

DRIVING HOME IN the dark from Fatumal's bungalow, my father was dazed by his harrowing nocturnal discoveries. He recalled that when she regained consciousness and opened her eyes she had flinched, as if she half-recognized him as the medical student who had sat with her by the stream in the hills. For his part, though he had sensed something familiar about her the moment he entered the bedroom, such was the disparity between the stinking, fleece-laden hut and the well-appointed, elegant bungalow that he wondered if he was having a vision. He still had trouble crediting that the poor hill girl and the rich man's wife were one and the same person.

Destiny has braided our lives together even as her hair was braided when I first saw her years ago, he thought. Though he was a married man in his mid-thirties, he was as fascinated by the grown woman as he had been by the girl in the Nawab's principality. He could not wait to talk to her privately, without Fatumal standing over her. He felt that the whole bungalow had had a disreputable atmosphere, in its way as sordid as the princely kingdoms in the hills. He wished he could somehow save her from the corrupt bungalow and her degenerate stepson. Even as he thought this, he scolded himself for taking interest—in a woman—as if he were still a carefree, adventurous medical student, rather than the devoted husband of a dutiful, pregnant wife and mother of his two daughters who was sitting up, patiently waiting for him in his own house. But, despite his best efforts and judgment, he could not push away thoughts of Rasil.

The seeds of his subversive thoughts about Rasil and her marriage were thus sown—or so I thought, listening to him in the Centre. Indeed, I conjectured that the groundwork for the Enchanted Period might have been laid right there in Fatumal's bedroom, with its charged and prurient atmosphere. Once again, as when he first met her at the rural dispensary, he was seeing her as a victim and imagining himself—perhaps unconsciously—as her rescuer.

❦

THE MORNING AFTER the shocking discovery, my father was surprised to get a telephone call in his office from Rasil. On her own, she confirmed the Jat Raja's account of her abduction and rescue, if hesitantly. He noticed a certain frankness and sophistication in her talk that made him wonder yet again how she could have been the hill girl he had known.

"I won't hide from you, Doctor Sahib, that I am an unhappy woman, that my days pass in sorrow and humiliation, in disgust at myself," she said.

"Those are harsh words," he said. "I hope you're only saying them because you're feeling poorly today."

"No, Doctor Sahib. That's the way I always feel. I am a helpless woman, not long for this world. You see, Rai Sahib has a snake in his own garden."

"You mean Ravinder?"

"Yes. The boy has no respect for me as a stepmother. A tyrannical, lecherous Nawab would not treat his maidservant the way he treats me."

"I have to say that I am skeptical that Auntie Rasil could have unburdened herself to you in one momentous telephone call to your office," I said, breaking into my father's mesmerizing account. "Perhaps you are misremembering."

"Your skepticism is ill-founded," my father said, confidently. "Though she telephoned me forty-five years ago, I remember the conversation as if it were yesterday. You know how it is in Indian offices—people are always coming in and interrupting—so she and I got everything said in a hurry, and on that particular day I remember that she telephoned me several times. There was no place in Lahore that we could have seen each other alone without starting a scandal, so the telephone was our best means of private communication. Lahore society was small, and everything about everyone was everyone else's business. Once the tongues started wagging, there would be no stopping them."

I stood up and poured us some sherry. I had recently introduced my father to the drink, even though it was contraband and thus fiendishly expensive in India, thinking that it was better for him than whiskey or brandy, both of which he found too strong.

Since I know the outcome, I thought, what can be the point of knowing all the details? Possibly he wouldn't be telling me any of this if he hadn't let down his guard because of old age. I wondered again if I should be protecting him from himself—preventing him from making confidences that he might later regret.

Still, now that we were in the middle of the story I could no more let go of it than I could drop a book that I was in the middle of writing. Perhaps I had no right to the story; after all, it belonged to him, and I had stumbled onto it inadvertently. But since I had started out as a sort of collaborator, I felt that it also belonged to me. Indeed, I felt that there was a symbiotic connection between the impropriety of his relationship with Rasil and the impropriety of my getting involved with it.

I handed him his glass. He took a sip, not so much with relish (it was a point of pride with him that he had gone to the grandest receptions in the British days and avoided alcohol as a matter of principle) as with a sense of duty (to his heart).

As he sipped his sherry, I paced back and forth in the cage of a room, feeling curious and wanting to hear more, and at the same time feeling that I was on the verge of hearing things that, as his son, perhaps I shouldn't hear. I was already feeling too much like a voyeur, seeing not only into my father's private doings but also into the private doings of Rasil and Fatumal and Ravinder.

"I was leery of getting drawn into Rasil's situation," he resumed. "But having heard what she had told me on the telephone, how could I remain disengaged? She was clearly being driven to distraction, and she was all but directly appealing to me for help. She had grown up to be a proud woman, and she couldn't have come out and said, 'Please save me,' but that was clearly what she meant."

"So what did she say?"

"She said that whenever Ravinder found himself alone in the house with her, he would try to grab her—try to touch her hair, bottom, or breasts. For a long time, she fought off his obscene advances as best she could. Then he started sneaking lewd letters into her dresser, among her underclothes."

"But why didn't she go to her husband, show him the letters, get the fellow thrashed and turned out of the house?"

"Son, I asked her the same question. She said that, although she had plenty of evidence against him—all the letters were written in his hand—she dared not go with it to Fatumal because she was convinced, as Ravinder must have been, that in Fatumal's eyes his sons could do no wrong, and that if he had to choose between Ravinder, his son and heir, and his wife, he would choose Ravinder, irrespective of the evidence."

"But she had his actual letters!"

"She was sure that Fatumal would not even look at them. He would simply dismiss her accusations as those of a plotting stepmother. She felt it was not beyond him even to cast her out as a Jezebel, as one would say in the West. The situation was made more dire by the fact that she had not given Fatumal a child. In our blessed country, when a couple is childless the wife gets the blame and, since Fatumal already had healthy sons, everyone thought that it was her fault that they didn't have a child. Anyway, she had none of the rights that a woman gets automatically when she gives her husband a child."

"Could he really have turned her out?"

"There was no doubting that she was actually frightened, but the threat was all in her imagination, although I couldn't have known it at the time. My later reading of the situation was that Fatumal had as much to fear from losing Rasil as she had to fear from losing him—his social position depended on his beautiful wife. But all I can tell you is that at the time that's how she saw things, and I therefore saw things as she did."

"So what did she do about the lewd letters? Did she just ignore them—and also ignore Ravinder?"

"I don't know about the letters, but, as she soon told me, there was no ignoring Ravinder."

"Ravinder has repeatedly forced himself on me, Doctor Sahib," she had told him. "When I resist, he beats me. There is nothing I can do—I am so afraid of him."

My father was furious and told her there was plenty she could do: she could go to the police and get Ravinder arrested, she could run away, she and my father could confront Fatumal together—or, better still, they could confront that stepson. "I could give him a good drubbing," my father said.

She dismissed all of his suggestions as impractical. My father had no legal standing with respect to her. The only people who did—Dr. Kaul, his father, and her own father—had all died in the meantime, and recourse to the police would give rise to public scandal, as would, even more certainly, my father's intervention.

My father felt impetuous enough to tell her, "Hang the scandals!" But he was in the government service, with a wife and children, so he said something equivocal—just enough to reassure her. "Surely your safety and happiness are more important than your good name."

"My good name is not worth anything," she said. "I don't care whether I live or die, let alone about my good name. The only things I'm living for are the children, Shoni and Varinder. They are so young, and they need me." She explained that Fatumal had kept his prenuptial promises to Dr. Kaul. In every way, he had proved to be a man of his word. Her half sister, Shoni, who was now about ten, was living in Fatumal's house and being brought up as their daughter. Indeed, Fatumal more or less treated Shoni as his own child, just as Rasil treated his younger son, Varinder, who was now about thirteen, as her own. These children were the only people in the world whom Rasil now had, her well-fed half brother having long since grown up and gone his own way. Rasil could never think of her own future without also thinking of the children. Varinder would always have his father, but if she weren't there Shoni would be at the mercy of the winds.

"You know, Doctor Sahib, in marital matters people always take the side of the man, so it would be Ravinder who would get the public sympathy, and Shoni and I would be out in the cold. And I would never be able to see Varinder again."

My father argued with her this way and that way, trying to refute her objections to taking some action against Ravinder, but, in the end, had to acknowledge that she was right and that there was nothing he could do. And yet throughout their conversation there was an undercurrent of appeal to him as a friend who had known her when she was a girl.

"It's not clear to me why she was burdening you with all her confidences when she must have known that, as a married man, as a family man, you couldn't afford to get involved," I said.

"I think everything had been bottled up in her ever since she got married, and she might not have survived if she hadn't had a shoulder to lean on."

"But she must have discovered the true character of Fatumal and Ravinder early on. Why didn't she turn to Dr. Kaul and his father back then? They seemed the kind of men who would have given her shelter. After all, they had rescued her and then taken her in despite her sullied name."

"She didn't feel that she could ask the Kauls to do more for her than they had already done. It was one thing to take a young, unmarried girl away from a police sub-inspector and give her a home, and quite another thing to take a married woman back from a 'good family.' As she pointed out, the attitude of our menfolk toward such matters is 'You belong to your husband and his family, and you must die with them.' Of course, there is no way of knowing whether the Kauls would have taken such an attitude, because they were never put to the test. But that is what she thought. Anyway, people don't like to hear or know about such matters."

"What matters? Incest, you mean?"

"Ravinder was her stepson, so technically it was not incest. I just mean anything that's sordid, that doesn't fit the picture of a 'good family.'"

"But Fatumal's was not a good family."

"They had money and position, so they were part of that small social set in Lahore, and people don't look too closely at

what skeletons a family has in their closet. They are too afraid
of exposing their own skeletons."

"Still, I don't understand why it should have been you that
she chose to lean on."

"What can I tell you, son? She felt connected to me. However she had changed, however she had been transformed,
somewhere inside her there was still that hill girl. Later, when
I got to know her better, I remember noticing that she had a
kind of reticence that suggested a secret past. She might have
sloughed off her old self like an old skin, but something of it
remained with her. Perhaps I was the only one who could have
sensed that, since until that nocturnal call from Fatumal that
was the only Rasil I had known." He drank a bit of his sherry,
wiped his mustache—which he had sported since he was a
young man—and went on, "That memory of her, you might
say, made me feel somewhat responsible for her. I certainly
recall the warm feelings her confidences evoked in me. She was
no ordinary woman. She was talking like one of us but telling
me things that were from another world. We know about the
perfidy of stepmothers and stepsons—our mythology is full of
that. But what she was telling me was all too real—rape by her
stepson under her own husband's roof. It was extremely disturbing, and yet, I have to say, not without its fascination."

❦

MY FATHER AND mother began running into Fatumal and
Rasil regularly at the Cosmopolitan Club, but, as my father told
it, the subject of Ravinder and Rasil's relationship was not
alluded to again, either by Rasil or by Fatumal. Whenever she
and my father met, she acted as if she had never confided in him.
He imagined she had decided to keep everything to herself and
present a brave face to the club and the world. That was just as
well, since he could not do anything to alleviate her suffering
and he didn't want to disturb my mother's peace of mind by
telling her that as a student he had been enamored of Rasil or,

indeed, that he and Rasil now shared a sordid secret. As he said, he had always lived his life straight as an arrow. He made up his mind never to see her alone. The two of them, however, could not refrain from surreptitiously exchanging looks now and again. Otherwise, as my father put it, "mum was the word."

The Cosmopolitan Club had a homey Indian atmosphere. Women either sat outside on the grounds watching their husbands play tennis or congregated in the Ladies' Section—a room off limits to men—where they knitted, embroidered, or played gin rummy. Many of the members of the club were Muslims, and if their womenfolk came to the club at all they observed strict purdah. In contrast, Rasil mixed with the men like a European. She was one of the few women to join men at the mixed bridge table and one of the first Indian women in the province to play tennis. Every time she walked onto the tennis court in a white sari, with racquet in hand, she created a sensation. She was often my father's partner both on the court and at the card table, and she liked my father to tell her when she made silly mistakes, so eager was she to improve her game and her play.

"She established an equally warm friendship with your mother, and so quickly that your mother thought that *she* had introduced *me* to Rasil," my father said. "The two women were brought together by Sheila, the wife of Basheshwar Nath Khanna, a tall, majestic Pathan and a man of the world. He and I had been friends since we were classfellows at Government College in Lahore, and, from the day of our marriage, your mother had been close to Sheila. When I'd kept back from your mother my encounter with Rasil at Fatumal's bungalow and our subsequent conversations, it never occurred to me that the two women would become good friends—that added enormously to my burden of keeping everything about Rasil secret. Then it so happened that, when your mother had been delivered of your sister Umi, at our house at 11 Temple Road, there was a sudden crisis. Your mother needed an immediate blood transfusion. She had given birth to your three sisters within a space of less than three years, and she was weak. Rasil happened to be on the spot. How that was, I can no longer remember—probably because she had become a friend of your mother. She immediately volunteered her blood. It matched your mother's blood type and was drawn by the attending lady doctor and passed on to your mother. At the time of the transfusion, the lady doctor must have said something to your mother, like that her life had been saved by her friend Rasil. It's the kind of hyperbole doctors often indulge in to comfort the patient. Of course, medically speaking, the blood of one donor is much the same as another's, and, anyway, the body is constantly making new blood. But your mother endowed Rasil's blood with certain supernatural powers, and forever afterward she thought of Rasil as her blood sister."

"I would have thought there would have been half a dozen relatives sitting around the house at the time, waiting for the arrival of the baby, any one of whom would have given the blood. Why would Rasil have been involved at all?"

"I don't remember. It could have been that the relatives in the house were shy of the needle. Giving blood was hardly known in Lahore. And Rasil came forward because she had no such inhibitions."

❦

ONE EVENING, SOME time after my father's surprising visit to Fatumal's bungalow and a month or so after Umi's birth, Fatumal approached my father in the clubhouse and asked him if he would take a turn or two with him around the grounds. My father preferred to keep his distance from him, but Fatumal was a club member, and so he did the courteous thing and followed him out.

"I won't detain you more than five minutes, Doctor Sahib," Fatumal said. Then he lapsed into silence, and it took him some time to continue. "I have skimped on nothing for Rasil, Doctor Sahib—English tutors and music masters, clothes and jewelry. I have given her everything before she has opened her mouth to ask for it. Which man wouldn't? She is beautiful, she is good with household duties, she is talented—she is excellent in the tongue of our emperor while at the same time excellent in our own music. Yet . . ." He again fell silent.

My father wanted to shake the fellow and ask him why he felt the need to boast about Rasil, when everyone who came into contact with her could surmise her exceptional qualities. Moreover, he did not feel comfortable talking to Fatumal about Rasil, for fear that he might be put in a position where he would have to lie overtly about what he already knew in respect to their marriage.

"You will be shocked to hear, Doctor Sahib, that I have a severe complaint against her."

My father fell back a step. The last thing he imagined was that Fatumal would have cause for any complaint against Rasil. He was wondering what that could possibly be, when Fatumal went on, "In my nine long years of marriage to her, not once has she performed her conjugal duty. In fact, our marriage has not yet been consummated."

My father was startled. Even as he admired Rasil for resisting the blandishments of the wretched man, he wondered how it was that Ravinder could force himself on her and Fatumal couldn't. Or could it be that that he wouldn't? For all my father knew, Fatumal loved her so much that he felt unworthy of her. In spite of himself, my father felt sorry for the man.

"It's not a medical problem in my competence, Rai Sahib," my father said at last. "That's probably not something anyone can help you with."

"I know, I know," Fatumal said, sighing and shrinking.

Even though my father found Fatumal's confession heartrending, he realized that the new unwelcome knowledge would make the prospect of seeing him day after day at the club even more awkward and distasteful than it already was. But there was no avoiding him, either in or out of the club— Lahore society was just too small. Anyway, he loved having

Rasil as his tennis or bridge partner, and, wherever she was, Fatumal was bound to be in the background watching.

My father gave Fatumal a chance to compose himself, and then walked with him back into the clubhouse.

✿

"DID RASIL FEEL any affection for Fatumal, or did she only have feelings of aversion?" I asked. "Was she tortured by the fact that she could not serve him as a proper wife?"

"These are not questions that Rasil could have answered herself, I think. What I can tell you is that I have wandered far and wide and I have lived by the light of our proverb 'In this world of ours there are people of all kinds and quality, but you should mix with them the way streams conjoin.' I have always been able to find some good qualities in everyone I have known, but it was hard to discover what they were in Fatumal. Certainly, no one liked him."

"I can't remember ever meeting Fatumal."

"I'm not surprised. After we left Simla in 1937, we saw little of Rasil and even less of Fatumal."

What marvellous luck to be put in the possession of the personal story of a kidnapped, ravished hill girl, I thought. And I called her Auntie. And if I had got to know her boorish husband I would no doubt have called him Uncle. The writer in me was mobilized, and, fleetingly, I worried again about being my father's Judas. Writers were notorious for spilling everything. I felt I must warn him against myself, because I wanted to be, in my own way, as open with him about my private thoughts as he was being with me.

"I wonder if you should trust me with your confidences about Auntie Rasil. Maybe you shouldn't tell me any more about things that you want to keep secret."

He laughed off my solicitude, as if my scruples made me more, rather than less, trustworthy. My worries began evaporating in the warmth of his laughter, like the morning dew under the sun.

III

THE SIMLA STAGE
IS CHASTE

I T WAS EVENING, AND ONCE AGAIN MY FATHER WAS sitting in my room at the Centre with his attaché case and resting his feet on the bed. He started reminiscing about Simla.

"In 1931, after two years of service in Lahore, I was invited to apply for an All-India job with the Red Cross. The position was that of organizing secretary for its antituberculosis fund. The fund was established to give thanks for King George V's recovery from the disease. The assignment was initially for only a year, but it could be extended. The salary was much better than what I was getting in Lahore and included a monthly relocation-and-house allowance to compensate for the high rents in Simla. I had long wanted to move out of Punjab service. It was a hub of provincial bureaucracy, crawling with backstabbers—subordinates trying to get ahead by doing down their superiors. Anyway, I wanted to make my mark in a bigger arena. I applied for the antituberculosis job and was selected. Like other All-India top officers and their families, we now started living half the year in New Delhi, the winter capital, and half the year in Simla." His tone suddenly switched, and he continued dreamily, "What heady times those were! I was young, fearless, and maybe even reckless, with an All-India job with the imprimatur of the King-Emperor. My mission was nothing less than to rid the country of one of the most devastating scourges. Moreover, your dear mother and I lived in the heart of Indian-British society, in as grand a manner as any Indians. Your mother never liked New Delhi—she found it cold and geographically too spread out—but she and I both loved Simla. Many of our Lahore friends and relations came up there for the summer, including Rasil. As a hill girl, she couldn't stand the heat of Lahore, and even though Fatumal could seldom be in Simla, because of his business interests in the plains, she was there all summer long. It was the most sought-after place to be in the hot season. The prominent Indians were invited to tea parties at the Viceregal Lodge as a matter of course. Your mother and I would be invited, and so would Rasil. She and I would play mixed doubles there, in full sight of English and Indian guests."

"So your romance began the first summer you were in Simla?"

"Oh, no—that happened in the second summer. But the first summer she was practically living with us like family, looking after your dear mother and Om, who was just a couple of months old when the family arrived in Simla. Your mother was in poor health." My mother had given birth to my three older sisters, Pom, Nimi, and Umi, and to my brother Om all within five years of one another, and before she had turned twenty-three. "My god, you should have seen how Rasil took care of your mother! No nurse could have done more for her. Your mother credited Rasil with all but saving her life—then, and also two years earlier, when Umi was born. Both the women felt that their lives were knitted together forever."

"But how did Mamaji and Auntie Rasil become so close? Mamaji was a traditional Indian woman without much schooling, and Auntie Rasil was a virtual memsahib."

"There was really nothing of the mem about Rasil. She had modern accomplishments but was basically a traditional woman. She wanted to be like your mother, while your mother wanted to be like her. It may interest you to know that your mother admired Rasil so much that, when we were in Simla, she parted her hair the same way and wore the same kind of sari, blouse, and shoes as Rasil did. Anyone looking at them would have thought they were sisters."

"But Mamaji would never have picked up a tennis racquet or sat down to play bridge with men."

"That's true."

"And Auntie Rasil must have stood out for being childless among other women, who must have all been mothers."

"But, remember, she was bringing up Shoni and Varinder as her own children. In fact, she doted on all children. She became a sort of second mother to your older sisters, who were all under ten throughout the six or so years we were in Simla. Shoni and Varinder grew up more or less alongside them."

"But I remember Pom, Nimi, and Umi saying that there was a certain amount of tension between them and Auntie Rasil. They said that although they always fussed over her as someone special, she was constantly showering them with presents and sweets, as if she craved their affection and couldn't take it for granted—felt the need to buy it, as it were."

"It could be that Rasil, not having a child of her own, was not as natural around children as, say, your mother."

"Are you sure you didn't discover your romantic feelings toward Rasil when you first got to Simla, or, for that matter, even before that, in Lahore?" In the beginning, I had had trouble speaking, even thinking, about the details of his romance. But as we talked about it more and more I had become freer with him. Even so, I had to maintain the illusion that we were discussing not my father, sitting next to me in my room at the Centre, but another person in another period. Indeed, so much had happened to our family since Independence, the Partition, and the resulting diaspora that I could scarcely believe that I had been born and had grown up under the Raj—a period as dead and gone for me as our life in Lahore.

"In Lahore, I certainly felt protective toward her. I wanted to save her from the rank goings on in Fatumal's house. But I never thought of her in a romantic way. Anyway, a hint of public scandal there would have been damaging to my career. I even warned your mother against getting too involved with Rasil. I always tried to keep my distance from extremely rich people. As our proverb has it, 'neither the friendship nor the enmity of the rich is agreeable.' But I felt sorry for Rasil, because she knew that everyone disliked Fatumal. Also, your mother was constantly being thrown together with Rasil because of her friendship with Sheila. I sometimes think that I would never have got involved with Rasil if your mother hadn't got involved with her first."

"But something must have changed once you got to Simla."

"I don't know what that could have been. What I do know is that all around Simla there were woods and ravines, secluded walks and hills where people had a kind of privacy unknown in Lahore. That was the beauty of the place—its lure. In Simla, I socialized with the British on an equal footing. I had British colleagues on my Red Cross subcommittee. Their outlook and morality were altogether freer than ours, and I felt liberated and intoxicated. Everything in Simla conspired to bewitch me."

❦

ALTHOUGH THE STORY of my father's romance seemed to occupy a private compartment in his mind, it of course took place in history. Indeed, he could scarcely speak about Simla without mentioning Sir John Lawrence, Lord Lytton, Lord Dufferin, and Lord Curzon, the nineteenth-century Viceroys, as if each of their Viceroyalties marked a distinct era. Annandale, the Gaiety Theatre, and Jakko Hill—some of the landmarks of his beloved Simla—also seemed to have a talismanic power over him. All these people and places were so familiar to him that he scarcely ever thought of explaining what part they had played in the formation of the Simla he remembered. As I tried conjuring that Simla, I got down from my bookshelf a few familiar books about the geography and history of the place, among them "Plain Tales from the Raj," by Charles Allen; "Simla: A Hill Station in British India," by Pat Barr and Ray Desmond; "Imperial Simla," by Pamela Kanwar; and "The Magic Mountains: Hill Stations and the British Raj," by Dane Kennedy, in order to refresh my memory about the history of the place. What follows is distilled from these books.

Seven thousand feet above sea level, Simla is situated in the northwest of the Himalayas, which extend for fifteen hundred miles along the northern border of the subcontinent. They are the source of sacred rivers, which irrigate the land in the plains and have always provided a livelihood to the peoples who live there. From ancient times, the Himalayas have been known as the playground of the Hindu gods.

Simla, a tangle of ledges and hills, ravines and cliffs, lies along a crescent-shaped ridge six miles long, whose concave side points south, toward the Punjab plains. To the east, Jakko Hill, the highest peak in the hill station, rises a thousand feet above the ridge; to the west are the lesser Observatory and Prospect Hills. Jakko Hill is famous for its population of white-bearded, black-faced apes, or *lungoors*, and its attendant colony of monkeys, the monkeys being associated with the Hindu god Hanuman, in whose honor there is a small shrine on the summit. When Simla was first settled, the ridge was surrounded by jungle, dense with deodar cedar, pine, fir, maple, horse chestnut, and giant rhododendron. Doves, thrushes, barbets, cuckoos, and hoopoes cooed, sung, and chirped in the trees. Lions, leopards, bears, deer, and jackals roamed freely. Lupines, geraniums, hill anemones, columbines, and pheasant's-eye grew wild.

It is said that, originally, Simla was only one mud hut and that a mendicant eked out a living there providing water to way-farers. Then, in the early nineteenth century, British military officers, while marching their Gurkha troops through the hills, camped on the ridge and were struck by its cool temperature and its extraordinary beauty. Soon, reports of its benefits as a sanatorium were abroad, and Englishmen ravaged by fevers, heat, and the hard life in the plains were trekking up there to convalesce. The first Englishman known to build a summer house in Simla was Captain Charles Kennedy, a political officer for the princely Hill States, who in the eighteen-twenties migrated from the heat of the foothills, where he lived, to the refreshing cool of the ridge and got a hundred or so local hill people to knock together a home for him out of rough-hewn timber. It is recorded that, in the summer of 1827, he had as his guest Lord Amherst, the Governor-General of India, who, together with the Emperor of China, was said to rule half the human race. In order to keep Lord Amherst in fine fettle during his visit, apparently a thousand coolies were mobilized to haul and carry his baggage and paraphernalia up to Simla. At the time, the only way to get there was over a fifty-eight-mile-long perilous dirt cart road that went up from Kalka, a dust bowl of a village in the foothills, twenty-one hundred feet above sea level. The road was not only subject to flooding and landslips but was also so narrow and tortuous, and snaked along so many cliffs and precipices, around a zigzag of hairpin curves, that no four-wheeled cart could travel on it. It could be negotiated only on foot or horseback, by ekka or bullock cart. A rider would fall to his death in a gorge if his horse took fright and lost its footing at the sudden appearance of a deer or a crow. Many Englishmen who were not horsemen or did not have the strong constitution for the arduous journey travelled in jampans, curtained sedan chairs supported on two parallel poles and carried by four coolies. Leaky inside, jampans wobbled and lurched, because the coolies often wore badly fitting slippers. (Later, women and children were carried up the cart road in doolies, a sort of covered wicker cot also borne by coolies.)

Lord Amherst's visit put Simla on the map, and he was followed a year later by Lord Combermere, the Commander-in-Chief and so the second-ranking Englishman in the country, who oversaw the construction of the first good road in Simla, which ran three miles around the base of Jakko Hill. By 1836, when Lord Auckland became Governor-General, Simla had a mall, or promenade, on the ridge, two bazaars below it, and over a hundred cottages, many of them clustered around Combermere's road, with drafty tin roofs but with names like Sunnybank and Primrose Hill. In due course appeared a bank and a billiard room, some British shops along the Mall, and Christ Church, a solid building in Tudor style. (The cattle market Boileaugunj, commemorated by Kipling, was named after the engineer who designed Christ Church.) Increasing numbers of wounded, exhausted, and superannuated military officers had settled in Simla; many of them indulged in drinking, gambling, and riotous living. A huge valley situated to the north of the Mall and shaded by pine, fir, and deodar cedars—named Annandale, possibly after a glen in Scotland—was developed into a recreational ground for horse racing, archery, cricket, tennis, badminton, and croquet. Sometimes it was used for fairs, with mock pony races, fortune-telling, and portrait painting; other times a wooden floor was laid over the ground, and it was used for outdoor dancing. Lord Auckland's sister, Emily Eden, a local resident, wrote this in her journal, in 1839, about one of the social events at Annandale:

> We dined at six, then had fireworks and coffee, and then all danced till twelve. It was the most beautiful evening; such a moon, and the mountains looked soft and *grave*, after all the fireworks and glare.
>
> Twenty years ago, no European had ever been here, and there we were with the band playing the "Puritani" and "Masaniello," and eating salmon from Scotland, and sardines from the Mediterranean, and observing that St. Cloup's potage à la Julienne was perhaps better than his other soups, and that some of the ladies' sleeves were too tight according to the overland fashions for March, &c.; and all this in the face of those high hills, some of which have

Jakko Road. Ca. 1865.

A view. Simla. Ca. 1865.

remained untrodden since the creation, and we, 105 Europeans, being surrounded by at least 3,000 mountaineers, who, wrapped up in their hill blankets, looked on at what we call our polite amusements, and bowed to the ground if a European came near them. I sometimes wonder they do not cut all our heads off, and say nothing more about it.

A stay in Simla came to be perceived by the English as an antidote to "too much East"—to the loneliness and isolation of life in districts and cantonments, where civil and military officers could find solace only in forlorn clubs; to the searing heat and dust of the plains, where even bullocks and donkeys balked at their tasks in summer; to the plagues, droughts, and famines that regularly visited the country; and even to the bewildering, alien native cultures. The English enjoyed everything about Simla—the mountain air and scenery, the sight of the perpetual snowline in the distance, and especially the thick fog that would settle in for days at a time, curling and creeping around the hills and houses, though without the acrid smell of burning coal so prevalent in London. To quote Emily Eden again, "There is a sharp, clear air that is perfectly exhilarating. I have felt nothing like it, I mean nothing so English, since I was on the terrace at Eastcombe." Simla seemed to have fostered from the beginning a feeling of make-believe among the English, who would even speak of it as Anglo-Saxon, although, as Emily Eden noted, the local hill people far outnumbered the English residents.

Calcutta had long been the year-round capital of British India, but the English had never flourished in its sweltering-hot climate and in its squalid physical conditions. Soon after the Mutiny of 1857, or the Great Rebellion, as the Indians call it, when India formally came under British rule, the British made Simla the summer capital. In fact, Sir John Lawrence, who was Viceroy from 1864 to 1869, and who initiated the move, refused to work anywhere except Simla in the summer. He maintained that, since the advent of British rule, the work of the government in India had greatly increased, flooding him with reports from districts all across the country and from various departments, like Agriculture and Commerce. On top of it, the government in India was now required to keep London abreast of everything that was going on in the colony. He and other English in India pointed to many advantages of having Simla as a capital, among them: its inaccessibility would prevent the natives from coming up and settling there; its local people were docile and pacific and would serve the establishment well; it was situated in the Punjab, which was the most prosperous part of India and had good drinking water; it was near the home of the Gurkhas, some of the most valiant soldiers in the British military; and it was better placed to control the unruly, warlike North-West Frontier.

Yet although Simla was a mere hundred and forty miles from Tibet, it was 1,176 miles from Calcutta and 1,112 miles from Bombay, to say nothing of the distance to Madras. Moreover, having the capital in Simla required the Viceroy, the Commander-in-Chief, and their staffs and servants to move out of Calcutta, bag and baggage, annually. That was such an enormous undertaking that as much as a month was spent moving each way, and by some estimates as many as ten thousand coolies had to be mobilized to haul all the files, documents, and other official and personal paraphernalia of the government up the cart road. From London, the Parliament and the Secretary of State, who was directly in charge of India, objected from the outset to the great expense of the move. Also, many people in Calcutta saw the move as a slight to their city. But later Kipling would ridicule their civic pride in his poem "Tale of Two Cities," with this line: "Because, for certain months, we boil and stew, so should you," adding, "For rule, administration, and the rest, Simla's best."

Simla proved to be so attractive to the government officers that each year they came earlier in the spring and stayed later in the autumn, until they tarried there for seven months of the year. Soon, the Lieutenant-Governor of the Punjab, the province's administrative head, had also moved his office there for the summer, and the princes of hill states were trouping there looking for property and official favors. Although from July to the middle of September Simla received on average forty-one inches of monsoon rain, making bedsheets and boots dank, tables and chairs sticky, and tin roofs leaky and clattery, that does not seem to have interfered with the English enjoyment of the hill station. The English residents would put on their formal clothes, cover up in mackintoshes or capes and galoshes, and set out on horseback, in jampans, and now also in rickshaws—outsized perambulators with canopies, pushed and pulled by four coolies.

William Howard Russell, a journalist for the London *Times*, who had been wounded in the Great Rebellion and was critical of the British rule, once asked an Indian in Simla what he thought of the British and reported receiving this answer:

> Does the Sahib see those monkeys? They are playing very pleasantly. But the Sahib cannot say why they play, nor what they are going to do next. Well, then, our poor people look upon you very much as they would on those monkeys, but that they know you are very fierce and strong, and would be angry if you were laughed at. They are afraid to laugh. But they do regard you as some great powerful creatures sent to plague them, of whose motives and actions they can comprehend nothing whatsoever.

Among these bewildered people were ayahs, cooks, and bearers, whom the sahibs had brought along with them from the plains, and a huge number of local attendants of one kind or another. For instance, a syce would run behind a sahib's horse and, the moment the sahib dismounted, would be there to catch the reins and then wait with the horse until his sahib mounted again. Similarly, the jampanis and rickshaw-wallahs would squat and smoke beside their conveyances as they waited for their sahibs and memsahibs to return from their engagements. In the vast

Lower Bazaar, which ran down a steep hill off the Mall in chaotic levels, shopkeepers, who sold fruit, vegetables, meat, walking sticks, and sandalwood boxes, slept above their shops and stalls, sometimes seventeen to a room, in conditions not much more sanitary or healthful than those in the plains. Indeed, the local drainage system was poor and the water supply insufficient. Then there were the ever-present Untouchables, who daily cleaned the commodes and latrines and swept the houses and roads. All the hill people and other natives, unless they were in attendance, had to stay out of sight—were not allowed to go up onto the Mall between four and eight, when the English residents went on their strolls.

With the arrival of Lord Lytton, who was Viceroy from 1876 to 1880, and his wife, the English Simla became a resort without parallel in the country. The Viceroy and Vicereine conducted themselves with panache. Then Lord Dufferin, who was the Viceroy from 1884 to 1888, and his wife built the Viceregal Lodge, a grand residence at the summit of Observatory Hill, reputed to offer the best all-around prospect in the hill station—the lodge solidified Simla's role as a glamorous summer capital.

All along, the society of the summer capital was structured on civil-service and military hierarchy, and only the top English officers moved there. Some of the lesser English officers, who were stuck in the plains, sent their wives to summer there, in preference to sending them home on a long sea voyage. These wives shared flats or lived in hostels. They served as hostesses and chaperones for young single women who came there in the hope of finding diversion and husbands. There was no shortage of single men. The bachelors attached to the military and civil establishments camped out in hostels or hotels, and organized themselves into societies like the Order of the Knights of the Black Heart. Although they respected and protected the virtue of the single women, perhaps because they didn't want or dare to compromise the women's chances of marriage, they seem to have been game for anything with the temporarily unattached married women. People frolicked, flirted, and philandered, and the place got a reputation for scandals. Indeed, there was a designated spot called Scandal Point, although the scandal for which it was named was fobbed off on the natives: it was said that there the Maharaja of the princely hill state of Patiala had kidnapped on horseback the daughter or wife of a Viceroy. The story was all the more memorable for being totally implausible.

As the settlement of English residents grew and became entrenched, there appeared in Simla hosiers, milliners, tailors, gunsmiths, haberdashers, saddlers, confectioners, watchmakers, wine merchants, perfumers, photographers, and grocers. Chinaware and furnishings were imported directly from West End stores, as were delicacies like jams and sauces from Crosse & Blackwell. Simla acquired the feel and look and all the accoutrements of a suburban English town. The men hunted, and the women wrote in their journals and in their letters home about their experiences, or sketched the scenery and the portraits of high government officers. Together, the men and women went on picnics, attended concerts, and had long formal dinners and balls lasting to the early hours of the morning—dressing for one another, men in tails and women in long gowns imported from London or Paris. In one year of the Viceroyalty of Lord Dufferin, there were twelve large dinners, twenty-nine small dinners, a state ball, a fancy ball, a children's fancy ball, six casual dances, two garden parties, two evening parties, and a charity fête. Kipling, who visited Simla regularly in the eighteen-eighties as a correspondent for the *Pioneer* and the *Civil & Military Gazette*, in his book "Plain Tales from the Hills" portrayed Simla as riddled with frivolity, jealousy, and intrigue. But he also understood the lures of Simla, even if his appreciation was always tinged with friendly mockery:

> Men say, who simmer in the Plains below,
> That Simla people frivol. Be it so.
> Let us admit that, as the Plains assert,
> The Maidens of the Mountain sometimes . . . flirt,

> While Matrons dance, and others, wilder still,
> Give picnics at the back of Summer Hill.
> And bold, bad sportsmen on a lottery-night
> Sit up till morning dims the candle-light.

Next to parties and sports, nothing, it seems, was dearer to the English heart than theatre. As early as 1838, the residents had formed an amateur dramatic company and performed half a dozen plays a season in the Gaiety, a stuffy little theatre just off the Mall. The plays were mostly farces and probably were not so much acted as performed in slapstick manner, with men dressing up as women, as was the norm then. For the audience much of the humor must have come from seeing people they knew well strut about onstage. In 1887, Queen Victoria's Jubilee year, the Gaiety was rebuilt, complete with an orchestra pit and boxes for the Viceroy, the Commander-in-Chief, and the Lieutenant-Governor, the third-ranking government officer in the hill station. On the opening of the new Gaiety Theatre, the following lines, ascribed to Kipling, appeared in the *Civil & Military Gazette*:

> Praise most yourselves—the Perfect and the Chaste.
> Why 'chaste' amusement? Do our morals fail
> Amid the deodars of Annandale?
> Into what vicious vortex do they plunge
> Who dine on Jakko or in Boileaugunge?
> Of course it's 'chaste.' Despite the artless paint,
> And Pimm's best wig, who dares to say it ain't?
> Great Grundy! Does a sober matron sink
> To infamy through rouge and Indian ink?
> Avaunt the thought. As tribute to your taste,
> WE CERTIFY THE SIMLA STAGE IS CHASTE.

The Gaiety Theatre was now well on its way to becoming an institution. Gilbert and Sullivan operettas were performed there, and Kipling himself acted on its stage.

For some time, tongas, two-wheeled carriages pulled by two horses, first with bone-rattling iron wheels and later with slightly smoother rubber tires, had been plying the cart road. In 1898, serious work was begun on a narrow-gauge railway, all that was practicable, from Kalka to Simla. It required laying rails through more than a hundred tunnels and was completed in 1903, when the summer population was thirty-five thousand, of which seven thousand were Europeans or Eurasians. The railway went into operation during the Viceroyalty of Lord Curzon, the most imperial and the hardest-working of the Viceroys. He had no use for Simla; neither did his American wife, who found the Viceregal Lodge as tasteless as the home of a "Minneapolis millionaire." Lord Curzon complained that Simla was too bustling and too public, that it was garish, idle, monotonous, and gossipy. The truth was there had already been too many hotels and too much foot and animal traffic, and the introduction of the railway only added to the congestion. Everywhere, wildlife was in full retreat. Only the monkeys and *lungoors* on Jakko Hill held their ground.

❧

IN ORDER TO get up to Simla in the nineteen-thirties during the waning years of the Raj, my father remembered, the family would take a regular, broad-gauge train from Lahore to Kalka. There they would transfer to the narrow-gauge train for the climb into the hills, the little hill train so unsteady and shaky as it twisted and turned along nearly a hundred hairpin curves that everyone had the illusion of climbing on rope ladders through the air up to heaven. Along the way, it would pass through the innumerable tunnels, creating great excitement for my sisters and brother. It also would pull in at a couple of small stations, where my father would buy the children freshly fried *pakoras* from the venders. Before eating the vegetable patties they would press them against their fingers, cheeks, and ears for warmth.

Even getting down from the train at the Simla station, down the slope from the ridge, was romantic. The air would be light and crisp and would be scented with deodar cedar. It would be completely free of petrol fumes, since everyone except the Viceroy, the Commander-in-Chief, and one or two other high officers was forbidden to drive a car in the hill station. People who drove up to Simla had to park their cars in a motor port near the train station. The family would hire donkeys and ponies for the children, rickshaws for the grownups, and coolies for the baggage, and they would set out uphill for their cottage, mesmerized by the clip-clop of hooves, the grunting and wheezing of the rickshaw-wallahs, and the chanting and muttered prayers of the baggage coolies as they tried to keep up their spirits. Their ascent would proceed at the stately pace of the private caravan of a maharaja.

❧

"THROUGHOUT THE TIME we were in Simla, we ran an open house for both your mother's family and mine," my father said during one of our conversations at the Centre. "Anyone who has a cottage in a hill station has an endless stream of visitors, and the bigger the cottage the more comfortable everyone can be. Babuji, Mataji, Bhabiji, along with so many of your uncles and aunts, came for long stays with us." Babuji and Mataji were my maternal grandfather and grandmother, and Bhabiji was my paternal grandmother. "They all enjoyed the salubrious climate of Simla."

"Did you have room for all of them?" I asked.

"Here in India, there is no question of room. All comers are accommodated as a matter of course. But the first summer we were there, in 1931, I jointly rented a big cottage with a close friend. The second summer, Fatumal and I together rented one of the most luxurious cottages there, called Windmere Lodge. The arrangement was advantageous to both of us. On my own, I could not have afforded the full rent—rents for big cottages in Simla were high—and Fatumal, by having a Class One government officer as his cotenant, got an entrée into government circles. Our two families lived together in Windmere for two consecutive summers."

"So you and Mamaji allowed yourselves to be indebted to a person that I know you disliked?" I asked.

"It's true I took against Fatumal in the beginning, but he became part of our circle. Everyone in the Simla club was. Anyway, we paid our full share of rent and household expenses, so there was no question of being indebted to anyone. Also, your mother was so close to Rasil that nothing was more natural than for the two women to share a house. It was just convenient all around. And I can tell you, son, your mother enjoyed Simla and Windmere very much. You should have seen her going along the Mall with Pom, Nimi, and Umi, and Om in the pram, and stopping every step or two to greet a colleague of mine or a friend of hers."

All of my sisters and brother were so small then, I thought. So maybe it was nice for my mother to have Auntie Rasil around, especially since my father was no doubt often either at his office or at his club.

"Did Mamaji go to the Simla club with you?"

"The Simla club was not a family club, like the Cosmopolitan in Lahore. It was not comfortable for her. She went with me only when there was some special function. But I recall that she did go with me to plays at the Gaiety Theatre. She particularly enjoyed Oscar Wilde's 'The Importance of Being Earnest.' She caught on to it quickly and laughed as heartily as the English."

"I would have imagined she wouldn't get much out of such a play—that the English dialogue, not to mention the wit and irony, would have gone over her head."

"You'd be surprised how much people can get out of plays just by watching, irrespective of the language. Anyway, the Indian government officers who liked going to such plays went just for the convivial atmosphere. We all liked seeing our English colleagues get on the stage. Your mother appreciated the spectacle in her own way. She was full of curiosity and observations. Everything was so new to us—we were so young."

I had to remind myself that we were talking about 1932, when my mother was just twenty-four, Rasil thirty, and my father thirty-seven.

"You must have your own memories of Simla," my father said.

"I do. They are of course from much later, and are anything but romantic."

❧

MY MEMORIES OF Simla date from 1947, when I was thirteen and my father's British Simla vanished with Independence and the Partition. Then Simla became the temporary capital of the new Indian divided state of East Punjab, and my father was posted back in the hill station. I lived there off and on for two miserable years, until I left for America for my education.

Since we had lost everything to Pakistan and become refugees, we couldn't even afford to take the train up to Simla and had to manage the trip from the plains in an old car. I recall one especially horrid journey through the hills. Even though my mother, knowing my tendency toward carsickness, had starved me for a whole day beforehand, I threw up at practically every turn of the climb. My father frequently pulled off the road to let me get out of the car and get some air and clear my head, but I was no happier outside in the cold than I was in the stuffy car. My mother, who was in the front seat with my baby brother, Ashok, the latest addition to the family, regularly passed me lemon drops to freshen my breath. My older sisters still complained that I smelt bad at the mouth and that if I just used my will power I wouldn't throw up. From the driver's seat, my father explained to them that my senses were finely balanced and that I shouldn't be berated for things over which I had no control. I lay, dizzy and half alive, on the laps of my older sisters in the back seat, breathing through my mouth to avoid the smell of mothballs that emanated from our woollen coats. When we finally arrived at the motor port, I felt weak and wobbly, and I couldn't get my ears to pop for a long time. I had to stand around in the chill while my mother and our servant, Gian Chand, took their time haggling with donkey-wallahs, pony-wallahs, and rickshaw-wallahs, who would carry us and our luggage to our government flat. My father never indulged in such bargaining; he was too Western-ized for that. Before the Partition, he would have agreed to give the coolies whatever they asked and later added a generous tip. But we were now refugees, and he had to, as he put it, lower his flag. Still, he held on to his dignity, standing aloof from the bargaining and pointing out to us children the hills and land-marks of his beloved Simla.

All the time I was in Simla, we lived in a flat on the second floor of a little two-story cottage called Erneston, at the bottom of a ravine. Inside, it was generally chillingly cold, smelled of must and mildew, and echoed like an empty shell. Living there, I always felt I had been exiled from familiar, snug Lahore to a campsite on a tundra. All of us were squeezed into three rooms, like so many mice. (The kitchen was in a separate little building.) In our house in Lahore, each of us children had had his or her own individual room, but in the flat we all slept in one long glazed veranda, curtained off to create cramped, improvised bed areas. There was one small coal fireplace in the flat, and we could afford to light it only in the evening. Then Gian Chand would dump some lumps of anthracite coal into the fireplace, light them, and vigorously fan the fire with a large bamboo hand fan. The whole room would fill with eye-smarting smoke, and we would have to open the windows and wait, coughing and tearing, until the fire was established and Gian Chand could cover the opening with a piece of tin to channel the smoke up the cold chimney. Eventually, the smoke would clear, and we would shut the windows as tight as we could against the drafts and huddle around the steady fire, the first warmth we would have felt all day. No matter how strong the fire, the room would remain mostly cold, and we would vie with one another to get our chairs close against the grate and toast our hands and feet, trying frantically to get the rest of our bodies to somehow warm up. During the monsoons and the winter, everyone would get colds and coughs and bronchitis, my mother suffering the most—she was subject to severe asthmatic attacks.

My older brother and sisters were still going to the same kinds of English-type school and college that they had gone to in the plains, and they were still enjoying extracurricular activities like tennis, badminton, and field hockey. But so backward were the conditions for blind people that, for many years now, there had been no school I could go to. In Lahore and Rawalpindi, the cities where my father had been posted for five years before they became part of Pakistan, there were *gullis* and lanes, parks and compounds where I could run around, bicycle, or while away the time with my cousins by flying kites, for instance. But in Simla I had no safe spaces where I could move on my own and no relatives of my age with whom I could play. I felt caged in and restless in Erneston. Even the peaks of the surrounding mountains seemed to close me in and asphyxiate my aspirations for independence and schooling.

All day long, I was left alone with my mother. Even in times of plenty, she had worried about not having enough money—about being driven out of house and home. And now, because of totally unforeseen political circumstances, that nightmare had come true. The fact that millions of refugees were all in more or less the same situation was little comfort to her. In our new state of affairs, she was as pessimistic (she would have said "realistic") about my father's ability to make ends meet as he was optimistic (he would have said "confident") about his ability to do so. I became an audience of one for all her anxieties. She would dwell on the facts that there were three more daughters to marry, without money for dowries, and that Ashok, who was three, had all his education ahead of him. She was sure that Om, who was now sixteen, wouldn't amount to anything, because he was interested more in acting and films than in books and college, and that I had never had prospects of any kind. As far as she was concerned, we were all destined to be lifelong dependents on our father, and he was four years short of his mandatory retirement at the age of fifty-five. My mother worried that he would not survive the shock of his retirement and the end of his government salary, and that she would be left a widow, and her only marketable skill, if it could be called that, was scrubbing pots and pans. Every part of our family had risen from poverty, and she seemed to think we were coming full circle: we would end up where we had started.

Still in my early teens, I became infected with my mother's dread. For once, it seemed to me much more realistic than the optimism of my father's gambling spirit. Not surprisingly, my Simla bore no resemblance to my father's earlier Simla or to the Viceregal Simla of nineteenth-century history.

❧

"I MYSELF HAVE been away from Simla for twenty-five years," I said to my father at the Centre. "Have you been back since we lived there?"

"Only once, four or five years ago, but I barely recognized the place. It was so dirty and overrun with crowds. Everywhere, trees had been cut down, and land had been built upon. Even the beautiful, secluded spots I remember from the good old thirties had been trampled upon and despoiled. It seemed that all of the Lower Bazaar had come up to the ridge."

"What took you to Simla?"

"I went to see my plot of land."

"I never heard about your plot. When did you buy it?"

"That's an interesting story," he said with a laugh. "I acquired it almost in my sleep, sight unseen, at the Cosmopolitan Club. Way back in the late thirties, I happened to mention to a friend at the poker table in Lahore that I had always wanted to own a small piece of ground in Simla—nothing big, just a place to park. I didn't think any more about it, but that friend in due course sent me papers and deeds for a plot. It wasn't much money, so, barely glancing at them, I sent him a check and executed the necessary papers without ever taking the time to go up and see the land. Then I misplaced the deed; as long as I had my house in Lahore, the plot in Simla just seemed like an extravagance. Still, I never missed a year's property taxes, which did not amount to much. When we were in Simla after the Partition, I didn't have the time to go and find the plot, but, later, every time I read that property prices there were going up by leaps and bounds, I thought of it as my equity in the hill station. I hoped that one day I would have enough money to build something there and, if I didn't, maybe one of you children would. In the sixties, I even had your uncle Romesh draw up a general plan for a wonderful cottage for us. As you know, he's always done architectural work for us free of charge, and he knows our family needs."

All the time we had been talking about Simla, I had not been able to summon up any agreeable memories about the place. But now that it seemed that we could have a cottage there, which might compensate my father, in small measure, for the loss of our house in Lahore, to my surprise some pleasant memories of the place came rushing into my head. I recalled the cedar-laden air and windswept silence of the hills, especially at night, when the faint, sad sound of someone singing or playing a flute in the distance would only underscore the silence.

"Did you and Uncle Romesh ever get anywhere with the project?"

"No, we never did. I never had enough money to build. I procrastinated—other things got in the way. I finally made a special trip to Simla and spent hours looking for the plot—going all around the place with a map—but there was no vacant land anywhere. The friend who had sold me the plot could be no help, because he had died long since. In the end, I went to the municipal authorities and discovered from the land register that he had certainly sold me a plot, but that it was just big enough to park a car and that someone had long since built on it. I had a good laugh over how literal-minded my friend had been."

"In your place, I would have been upset!"

"It does no good to get upset in our blessed country. What could I have done? To get the plot back would have involved a lot of legal fees and a court case, and ultimately I would have spent a lot of money and have had nothing to show for it. Anyway, the Simla I remember, and even the Simla you children remember, have gone the way of so many precious things. We can remember and talk about our Simlas but can never revisit them."

"I think I'd like to go up to Simla one day and see for myself what havoc all the changes have wrought. I'm sure there are some hills that haven't been built upon and which have remained pristine."

"That must be so, but your going there would take some careful planning. Getting accommodation there now is difficult. You would probably have to book a hotel room months in advance."

I was never able to plan far ahead, with the result that, since leaving Simla some fifty-five years ago, I have never been back.

"You know, for all our talk about Simla, I still can't picture your life there," I said.

"What kinds of things can't you picture?"

"For instance, I have no exact picture of what Auntie Rasil was like in those days."

He was slow to respond. "You ask too much of me, son. It's not easy to describe someone one has loved." He became uncharacteristically silent, drummed his fingers on the attaché case, and sort of hummed to himself, as if he were pondering something. He abruptly asked, "How is your work on the Mahatma Gandhi book coming along?"

"O.K.," I said, wondering if he wanted me to drop the subject of Rasil, along with Simla. I myself was bedeviled by contradictory wishes. In some ways, I found the whole subject excruciating and wondered yet again if it was appropriate for him, as a father, to discuss his affair of the heart with me, as his son. Yet, through the artifice of "Hill Girls" and through our conversations, he had vouchsafed to me so many tantalizing details about his affair that for him to stop now was frustrating. Also, I worried that, if my curiosity were left unsatisfied, I would be tortured by all manner of conjectures and speculations. Of course, if he had wanted to, he could have extricated himself at any time from the whole awkward business by cutting short our conversation and leaving for home. That would be what I would have done in his place. But, then, I was as closemouthed with him about my own affairs of the heart as he had been open with me. I felt guilty about my silence but rationalized our different approaches by telling myself that I had a right to know his story, since it was in a sense part of my own history, but that it would do him no good to know any more about mine than he already knew from necessity or from his own observations. I would only be transferring the searing pain of my own losses onto him, and we were so close I imagined that if he knew about my pain he would feel it as his own. I had all along felt that the best thing I could do was to keep his old age as trouble-free as possible. He had had more than his share of life's burdens. As the head of the whole Mehta clan, he had helped to put every last member of the extended family on his or her feet. He had brought up his own seven children and, as a good Indian parent, got them all married—I was the only exception—and settled, and all that in a poverty-ravaged country, through the turmoil of India's long freedom struggle, the Second World War, and the Partition.

My father stood up and said that it was getting late. "I wish you'd come home with me, son. Your mother's always asking why we don't see more of you."

It was true that I saw less of my mother than I would have

liked to, mainly because, unlike my father, she seldom ventured out in the evenings. She hardly ever went to the club,
feeling that it was an unnecessary expense—a luxury appropriate for a breadwinner but not for a wife. She preferred to stay
close to home and while away the evenings with her women
friends in their Delhi neighborhood, Nizamuddin Colony. She
was popular there—indeed, was the president of the women's
association. On comfortable evenings, she and her friends
would go for walks around the Tomb of the Moghul emperor
Humayun. Its grounds served as an informal gathering place
for the whole colony.

"I'll come another night," I said, feeling guilty for not
spending all my time in Delhi with my elderly parents. But
thinking about their reduced circumstances, their valiantly
carrying on in their modest refugee house, made me sad. If they
were still living in Lahore, their lives would have been much
richer and more fulfilled. As it was, they thought them fulfilled
and seldom looked back.

As my father drove off in his twenty-five-year-old beat-up
wreck of a Vauxhall, which he had constantly to have repaired,
but which he had never had enough money to replace, I tried
to see his life in a different light. He was lucky to have
acquired a claim to a plot of land in Nizamuddin. The colony
was originally developed on a sort of scrubland by the government for the refugees streaming in from Pakistan, and my
father's plot, four hundred yards square, had been a part of his
small compensation for his lost land and house in Lahore. He
had been able to build a small house on it with the dribs and
drabs of money he earned in America, from Mrs. Clyde and for
giving lectures. The house, though a pale shadow of our Lahore
house, provided him with a roof over his head. Moreover, since
he acquired the land, Delhi real-estate prices had risen perhaps
a hundredfold, and Nizamuddin had become one of the city's
most elegant neighborhoods. But none of that could compensate him for the intangible, now remembered things he had
lost in Lahore: the thrill he felt every time he drove past the

landmarks of his youth—Central Model School, Government College, King Edward Medical College, Lawrence Gardens—or the lift he felt when he ran into his old friends or relatives, whom the Partition had since scattered to various cities in India. Indeed, like the rest of the human flotsam and jetsam known everywhere as "displaced persons," he was cut adrift from a thousand and one old associations.

As he liked to say, he now relied on the light of his memories to guide him through old age and his diminished place in the world. Just thinking that shifted my perspective on his confession, if that is what it was, and made the whole question of what was or was not proper for me as a son to know seem irrelevant. What was important for him was to somehow keep his memories alive.

IV

THE ATTACHÉ CASE

A S MY FATHER REMEMBERED IT, HIS ENCHANTED Period lasted from the beginning of the summer of 1932, when the family moved into Windmere Lodge, to December of 1933, three months before my birth. The phrase "Enchanted Period" had become our code for his dalliance. It allowed us to put the potentially explosive material into the distance and so to speak about his illicit romance with a minimum of embarrassment.

"During the Enchanted Period, I was so possessed by Rasil that you might say I hardly had any will of my own," he said. "In reality, we did not spend all that much time together. In the winter, she was in Lahore, and I was in New Delhi, and we could meet only when something took me to Lahore. In the summer, I sometimes had to go on tour. Even when we were both in Simla, opportunities for seeing each other alone were not all that plentiful. But, whether we were together or apart, I was possessed by her. We wrote to each other—she much more than I, though I tried to keep up my end of things."

"What happened to all of those letters?"

"She burnt mine, but I saved hers."

"I suppose they got lost with everything else in the Partition."

"Oh, no. Long ago, I had entrusted them to Prakash for safekeeping, in a sealed envelope. Since he was living in Bombay most of the time, they survived the vicissitudes of the Partition." Prakash was my father's nephew. He was the only other member of the older generation of our extended family who had shown any interest in writing. Indeed, as a young man he had gone to Bombay hoping to have a career as a film-script writer. His plans hadn't worked out, and he had ended up as a customs officer. It struck me as somehow fitting that my father should have chosen him, of all people, as the custodian of the letters.

"Does Cousin Prakash still have the letters?"

"My instructions to him were to return them whenever I asked for them or burn them in case of my death. Lately, with you taking interest in my story, I wanted to look at them again, so I retrieved them from him. I have been reading them and reliving the Enchanted Period."

My writer's imagination was inflamed. I saw in the letters a repository of clues to a lost history, not only my father's but also perhaps Simla's. But what right did I or anyone else have to read them? How would I feel if someone read my love letters? I had my own little secret trove. Even if my father should allow me to read them, how could I, as my mother's son, handle the guilt of reading them? Anyway, wouldn't reading them turn me into a Peeping Tom—a man who was made blind for looking where he shouldn't have? In fact, there is a universal inhibition against a child's curiosity about what goes on in his parents' bedroom. Yet, even as the son in me struggled with filial obligations and inhibitions, the writer in me had trouble renouncing the unseemly wish.

"Where are the letters now?" I asked and immediately regretted my blunt question.

I must be more tactful if I ever want to see the letters, I thought.

"The letters are right here," he said, tapping the attaché case.

So he's been carrying them here in the evenings, I thought. Possibly he wants to show them to me but has conflicts about it that are not unlike mine.

Even as I was debating whether to ask to see them or to put them out of my mind once and for all, he undid the latches, opened the attaché case on his lap, and, from under his change of clothes, started pulling out the paraphernalia of an old man—old counterfoils from checkbooks, old clippings, used airmail envelopes, a gold watchband, and an empty Harrod's plastic shopping bag. Then he brought out a packet of letters loosely tied with a string.

"Here they all are, saved for forty and more years," he said, untying them and flipping through them. They were in envelopes of many sizes and colors; some without envelopes at all.

I wondered what he was going to do with them. Hand them over to me just like that, without any hesitation or restrictions? That hardly seemed possible. But it also seemed that that was what he had in mind, for why else would he have taken the packet out? I waited for a long, suspenseful moment.

He tied up the letters, put the packet back in his attaché case, put back the paraphernalia and the change of clothes, and latched the case shut.

That is the right thing for him to do, I thought. I decided I would squelch my curiosity about the matter.

My father announced that he was off to the club to take his hot shower. He said that he hadn't been there for some evenings, and his friends must be wondering what had happened to him.

I walked him to his car with the attaché case.

What if he misplaces it in the club, I wondered. I should have made him leave it with me. He would know that I would never look at the letters without his express permission.

For some days, although he always brought along his battered attaché case on his evening visits and kept it close to him, I never knew whether or not it still contained the packet of letters. He did not bring up the subject, and I felt that I shouldn't. Then, one evening, without any preliminaries, he opened his attaché case, rummaged through it, and brought the packet out again.

"I think, son, that you should take charge of the letters now and keep them for me until I decide what to do with them," he said, handing the packet to me. "If I should die before I make up my mind, then your instructions will be the same as those to Prakash: to burn them without letting anyone ever read a line of them."

I held the packet gingerly, with blood rising to my face, and then stored it in my briefcase next to my manuscript, intending to carry it back with me to the United States for safekeeping.

Auntie Rasil probably thinks that the letters have long since been burnt, I thought. She would surely want them destroyed. And how would my mother feel if she knew that I knew anything at all about the affair, let alone that the letters have survived it and that my father has entrusted them to me? I wondered if my father, had he been younger, would have thought that entrusting the letters to me was a betrayal of, in different ways, both Rasil and his wife. But then I found myself doing a quick about-face and giving myself over to a certain amount of perhaps self-serving rationalization. The affair was long in the past. After it was over, my parents had had four more children. (The next to last, a son, had died when he was still a baby.) Their marriage always seemed to me to be better than most. Could it be that the letters were nothing more than a record of a dalliance that had succeeded only in strengthening their marriage? Anyway, since I did not plan ever to read them, what possible harm could my having them do to anyone?

"Why did you preserve the letters for so long?" I asked.

"They were a remembrance of such a happy period."

"You mean of you and Auntie Rasil?"

"Yes, but also of your dear mother. I tell you, the two women loved each other."

"Mamaji must have stayed friends with Auntie Rasil only because she must have sensed her own weakened position and so thought that that was her only hope of winning you back." Without my being aware of it, the mere possession of the letters had worked some mysterious power on me. Instead of talking to my father as a neutral observer, as I had been all along, I was now talking to him like a partisan of my mother.

"There was no question of winning me back, because I never intended to leave her," my father said.

"She couldn't have known that, and I wonder if you necessarily knew that at the time," I said.

"But in her heart of hearts she knew that I was a family man—that I would never let anything come between me and my children," he said.

"But what about between you and her?" I said. "I can't forget that you were disappointed in your arranged marriage to her. You thought that you were getting a wife who was educated, English-speaking, and musical. Then you found out after the wedding that she did not have any of those attainments. If you'd known that at the outset, you probably wouldn't have married her. I even wonder if you fell for Auntie Rasil because she had the particular attainments that you had dreamed of having in your wife. In Mamaji's place, I certainly would have thought that and worried over it."

I can only explain my boldness in questioning my father's interpretation of his own motives and intentions by the fact that I had already been his biographer. In talking to him for that book and in probing his past through his letters, to my mother among others, I had acquired a certain knowledge and been able to take certain liberties with him, unheard of in an Indian son. I sometimes even fancied that I perhaps knew more about the springs of his actions than he himself knew.

"But in your haste to understand a difficult situation you are forgetting how much your dear mother has always meant to me," he said calmly. "You couldn't possibly know how I adored her from the moment I brought her home as my bride."

"Doesn't that sort of beg the question of the two women's real feelings for each other, though? You might think they were close—they might even have put on a credible semblance of loving each other—and yet they could have been boiling inside with rage and jealousy. Certainly, once Mamaji found out about your enchantment, she could not have done more than tolerate Auntie Rasil. I myself cannot conceive of her dealing with the situation in any other way."

"You don't understand the mentality of a Hindu woman. Anyway, all I can tell you is that her behavior toward Rasil was impeccable—as was her behavior toward me."

"Are you sure your memory is not playing tricks on you?"

"Now that I think about it, once your mother did threaten to leave me. That was early in the Enchanted Period. As it happened, Babuji and Mataji were then staying with us in Simla and were sitting downstairs—your dear mother was with me upstairs in the bedroom. She had just found out about Rasil by opening a letter from her with the steam from a teakettle and then gluing it back. She said, through her tears, 'I want to separate from you and go back to Lahore with Babuji and Mataji. You must return my dowry.'"

"Did Babuji know about Auntie Rasil? And would he really have taken Mamaji back?"

"Once the cat was out of the bag, so to speak, there was no way of keeping the in-laws in the dark. They have their own way of finding out such things—the daughter confides in the mother, the mother confides in the father. But there is all the difference between such confidences and anyone acting on the basis of them. Certainly, Babuji would have never taken his daughter back once she had gone to her new home. He would of course have given her shelter for some time, and with his help she might have been able to manage things on her dowry money, but eventually he would have told her that she must go back to me—that a Hindu woman's destiny is with her husband, through fire and water. Your mother knew that as well as I did."

"So what did you do when she threatened to leave?"

"I said to her, 'I will somehow raise the money and make your dowry whole. But remember that once you leave my protection, I will never take you back.' I spoke so emphatically and with such determination that she backed down. After that, your mother redoubled her efforts to see only 'good points' in Rasil—to try to admire and love her like her own sister."

"So what you are saying is that you cornered her, gave her no choice."

"It was the system, not me, that gave her no choice. I think that if she had stopped to think she would have realized that herself. But she was overwrought, and I thought that the only way to bring her back to her senses was to be firm."

"It sounds to me like, once she found out about you and Auntie Rasil, she was only putting on a show of affection for everyone's sakes."

"I think her friendship with Rasil was genuine. It might not be understood today, especially in the West, but at that time, in Simla, it all seemed quite natural."

"How is that? What's so different about then and now?"

"I'm talking about a period when Muslims routinely had several wives and even Hindu Punjabis sometimes took more than one wife, when a widow of one man became the 'woman of the sheets' of his brother. I'm not suggesting that these things happened among our class of people, but that was the cultural background nonetheless."

"Knowing Mamaji, she could have been friends with Rasil and still hated her. She's always had a way of, as we children used to say, 'walking in opposite directions at the same time.' One minute she would be scolding a servant, but, if she suddenly realized that he might quit, then she would lavish him with praise. Her switch would be done all in one breath, as if she saw no contradiction in her behavior. We children used to laugh about that trait of hers, and I remember sometimes you used to join in with us. I now think that that might have been her way of coping with her general insecurity over being married into, as she used to say, 'the house of demon Mehtas.'"

"I know she always spoke of the hot tempers of 'the demon Mehtas.' Her side of the family, with the exception of Babuji, are all gentle Milquetoasts, but I think that's because they grew up in fear of Babuji's stick. He mostly did no more than brandish it, but, on a rare occasion, he was not above using it, even against his own wife. His children grew up hearing him say, *'Laton ke bhut, baton se nahln mante.'"*—"Demons who deserve kicks cannot be controlled by words." "But that's not and never has been the Mehta way. We may have fiery tempers, but they boil over and are defused in minutes."

"And yet your threatening to turn her out would"—I hesitated—"strike some people as brutal, especially since all the right was on her side." I resorted to the subterfuge of "some people" to soften my remark.

"You are right, son, but this is all in hindsight. I think I was only threatening in order to scare her out of doing anything rash—anything that might be harmful to her and our children. She knew as well as I did that the door of my house could never be closed to her. But instinctively I felt that our problems should be solved between us, not appealed to Babuji and Mataji sitting downstairs. At the time I was flushed with anger, and you might say I felt cornered in my turn. I grew up hearing Lalaji say, 'Never corner a tiger.'" Lalaji was his father. "But your mother, perhaps, never learned that lesson."

"She must have been driven to great depths of sorrow and anger to corner you. Surely her behavior is excusable."

"Of course, son. And it was probably prompted by her imagining that I would leave her and run away with Rasil, something that, as I told you, I would never have done."

"But how was she to know that? Any woman in her situation would have thought that. No wonder she was terrified out of her mind."

"That's all true. But you know, son, that in those days there was no such thing as divorce in our country, so there was no question of my running away anyhow."

"But I am sure there were some wives who were just abandoned."

"There wasn't a single case of that kind of thing in the history of the Mehta family, but of course that fear has been the lot of a Hindu woman since time out of mind. And your mother has always been ruled by fear. In that, she's just like her whole Mehra clan, and different from us Mehtas, who don't know what fear is. As a result, the Mehras, to get their way, have to do everything in a surreptitious fashion. I recall at the time happening upon a letter from your mother to her astrologer in which she, Mataji, and the astrologer seemed to be conspiring to put a hex on Rasil, in order to break up my romance with her. As I read the letter, I became angry and unjustly compared your dear mother with Rasil, the fairer one: How direct, how sincere, how warm, how generous, how dedicated she is compared with the mother of my children, I thought. Those thoughts were prompted by rage at your mother's superstition and at her behaving like Mataji, who did everything behind Babuji's back. Mataji had good reason to be afraid of Babuji, but I felt that there was no reason for your mother to be afraid of me. She knew from the day of our marriage that I was a straight shooter."

"I can see reasons for her to be afraid of you that have nothing to do with the fear of Babuji that she might have grown up with. The mere fact that you are a man would have been frightening enough."

"Well, well, well," he said, laughing. "There are men, and there are men. She knew that my anger is just like a little thunder and lightning that claps and flashes, and then passes over without really doing any harm. If at any time during the Enchanted Period I thought of not being at her side, the faces of Pom, Nimi, Umi, and Om would appear before my eyes. How could I ever leave them?"

"She might have known that at one level and not known it at another."

"Maybe you should read the Red Letters one day, so that you can have a full picture. Although you seem to intuit your mother's point of view, you don't seem to understand Rasil. She was incapable of hurting your mother."

I was bowled over by his suggestion, even though it was deferred indefinitely to a distant "one day."

He went on, "On the one hand, I wish that the letters had not survived—that they had been burnt, as both Rasil and your mother would have wanted. Then the question of anyone reading them would never have arisen. On the other hand, I am glad that they survived as a sort of footnote to history. But I don't mean to make any special claims for them—after all, they merely chronicle a few moments in a private life. Still, they are some kind of a record, however slight, of a vanished world."

"What world are you thinking of?"

"The world of the British in India. As you know, the British could not have ruled or stayed without inducting some Indian officers into the government. The unspoken condition of this status was that we native officers would be beyond reproach, but that basically meant beyond corruption. What we did in our private lives was our business, provided we behaved discreetly and avoided the taint of public scandal."

"Then, was your romance of no concern to your British superiors?"

"The British certainly didn't think that their carrying on romantic affairs compromised their respectability. So how could they worry about what their Indian subordinates did? Their relaxed attitude toward such things rubbed off on some of us Indian officers. All of us Class One officers imitated the British in one way or another. After all, we officers dressed like the British, and clubs and the tennis, bridge, and poker we played there were all introduced to India by the British."

"Do you know of other romances like that of you and Rasil?"

"Not many. But, then, such things were kept private. I doubt if there was anyone even in our club who knew about Rasil and me."

"I wonder how you would really feel if I were actually to read the letters—I mean, one day."

"I've been thinking that you might even have a right to them, as my biographer. I can never forget how you took private moments in my life and transformed them—made a book out of them. So you not only gave them significance but also provided justification for things I did or did not do. Maybe, if your book hadn't existed, I would have seriously thought about destroying the letters, even now."

Fleetingly, I wondered if the unspoken part of what he was telling me was that, if he ever permitted me to read the letters, he might want me to write that "footnote to history" that he had spoken about. The idea was daunting. How could I find justification, as he called it, for his conduct in this particular instance, since it must have hurt my mother? But then I told myself that a good chronicler should not be an advocate, a judge, or a prosecutor. He should only observe and record and let his readers draw their own conclusions.

"But the book about you has already been published, and I can't imagine revisiting the story of your Delhi-Simla job," I said. "Anyway, there is no obligation that a book about anyone should be as complete as the life. I was writing a biographical portrait of you—an artistic rendering of your life—not a full-scale biography."

"I of course understand that. But wouldn't your portrait of me have been different if you had known about my dalliance with Rasil?"

"But I could never write openly about Rasil and you as long as Mamaji is alive."

"You mean, as long as any of the three of us are alive," he said. "On second thought, I should have long since burned the Red Letters." He seemed to be waking up to the enormity of having preserved them in the first place and then of handing them over to me with the suggestion, however oblique, that I could write about them one distant day. Then he did one of the many shifts that were characteristic of all our discussions about the Red Letters. "They got saved because in the back of my mind I always had the idea that they would form the basis of my novel about Rasil. But I procrastinated, year after year, and now it's too late." He hurried on. "I can't tell you, son, how fantastic a heroine Rasil would have made. Just think of her origins, her abduction, her rescue and transformation, her cutting a figure not just in Indian but in British high society. Is there not a romantic novel in that?"

He was talking as if I could read the letters and continue with the novel we had started together—or was he? My mouth went dry. He thinks like a writer, I thought. To a writer, all is grist for the mill. "But for the novel to work, we would have to know a lot more than what would probably be contained in any love letters," I said.

"What do you have in mind?" he asked.

"We couldn't just write summaries of big events the way we did in 'Hill Girls,'" I said. "If we said Rasil was abducted, a reader would expect to see the police sub-inspector in the act, follow him to where he took her, see what he did to her, know how she reacted and how she was rescued. We would have to work out the sub-inspector's motives, his background, his character—God knows what else."

"Well, well, well. Such things about Rasil's life I never knew—she never talked about her kidnapping. They could only be a matter for speculation."

"Or, rather, for imagination."

"As I told you when we first embarked on 'Hill Girls,' my style is that of writing medical reports—of writing truthful accounts—so I wouldn't want anyone to make up things about Rasil."

"But if a novel were written with Rasil as its heroine, she would be a fictional character, and fiction has its own truth and logic."

"Then such novels are for writers like you. My kind of writer is best telling the unvarnished truth. To me, nothing is more sacred in my old age than my memories. I wouldn't want them to be tampered with for the sake of just making a good yarn."

He took his feet off the bed and made as if to go, saying, "All our conversations about Rasil are just between you and the lamppost. In talking to you, I have been dreaming aloud, so to speak. If you ever read the Red Letters, lock them in your heart. No one in the world should know about them. I have my children, my grandchildren, to think of. I want them to have good memories of me. I want them to remember me as an honorable man." He abruptly intensified his backpedaling. "I don't even want you to read the letters. I don't want you to think ill of me. I just want you to keep them safe until I can think through the whole problem of what to do with them when I'm gone."

"Reading the letters would never change how I think of you—how I will remember you," I said.

"In the end, son, I've learned it's more important to be moral than clever, though I know that, as an Oxford man, you'd think otherwise."

"Actually, I don't," I said. "I'm of your opinion."

"I like to think that even during the Enchanted Period I did not lose my sense of balance: that I put the happiness of my family before my temporary happiness, before Rasil's happiness, that my involvement with her was based on her enriching company, our love of music and tennis, our physical attraction—surface things rather than deep, abiding things like raising a family. I did not feel sad when the Enchanted Period ended. It was just a phase, an aberration. In fact, I have been truly sad very few times in my life: when Lalaji died while I was away in America, when I found out your mother's education had stopped with the fourth standard, when you went blind, when the Japanese bayoneted Krishan to death"— Krishan was his youngest brother—"in the Second World War, and when my firstborn was delivered of stillborn babies. For the rest, I have met the challenges of life as they came along and tried to be philosophical."

He started putting on his shoes. "You will remember that, when I used to visit the refugee camps after the Partition, I had to take down histories of refugees," he said. "Everyone who had lost property felt the same way as I did. There was a kind of aching absence that could never be compensated for. I feel a bit like that about the absence of Rasil from your book about me."

When he went home, he took his attaché case with him, but not the Red Letters, which remained safely in my briefcase.

❦

UNTIL I STARTED working on "Daddyji," in 1970, I had thought of my father only as a parent, as a superior being. But when I was talking to him for the book, I started seeing him also as a person with his own foibles and insecurities. In fact, he was so free with me in talking about his anxieties and missed opportunities that sometimes he seemed to speak to me as if I were his contemporary. For my part, I overcame the shyness of a son and peppered him with questions—in conversation when we were in the same city and in correspondence when we were not. But later, in preparing the manuscript for publication, first in *The New Yorker* and then in book form, I assumed a protective, almost parental role toward him and, for reasons of discretion, propriety, or taste, carefully edited out many of the things he had told me.

In 1972—two years before our conversations at the Centre—my father happened to be in New York when I received from the publisher my first bound copy of "Daddyji." He hadn't yet read the *New Yorker* articles, which had come out just before the book arrived. I rushed it over to him at 1 Fifth Avenue, thinking that he would be as excited as I was and take pleasure in holding the result of the seemingly endless streams of telephone calls, letters, drafts, revisions, and proofs that I had inflicted on him.

He was in his room alone, and I ceremonially handed him the book. He looked through it quickly and sat down heavily.

Rather than being elated, he was uncharacteristically dejected. He caught his breath and demanded that I promptly get the publisher to withdraw the entire edition.

I was stunned. I asked him what possible fault he could find with the book.

"I was just telling you all those stories as a father," he said. "I never imagined that they would be printed like this."

"How can you say that, Daddyji? I don't know how many times you read and commented on the drafts and proofs."

"I know, I know," he said. "But—until this minute—I didn't realize what I was doing. Seeing these stories between hard covers has given me one of the worst shocks of my life. You must get your publisher to burn the whole edition, whatever the cost. We'll simply have to reimburse them, even if we go bankrupt doing so."

After I had recovered somewhat from my own shock, I thought I sort of understood his reaction. There was a difference between revising chapters piecemeal, filling gaps in narration and amplifying this scene or that, and seeing the whole book in its final form, with no chance for revisions or second thoughts. I told him that I sympathized with his feelings—that many people were unhinged by seeing the record of their private feelings, thoughts, and doings in print—but that the discomfort was short-lived.

"You don't understand," he said. "If the edition is not withdrawn, Gaurev may be kidnapped, and we will have his blood on our conscience." Gaurev was his grandson by my third sister, Umi.

The idea was so bizarre and fantastical that I groaned. To humor him, I asked him, "What in the book could possibly cause you to have such dire apprehensions?"

In a lawyerly fashion, he pointed to a passage concerning the theft of a necklace from around the neck of my great-grandmother (his paternal grandmother) while she was sleeping.

"The thief, whoever he was, must be long dead!" I cried. "How can what happened so long ago lead to a kidnapping now?"

"The identity of the thief was no secret from Lalaji, though there was nothing he could do about it," my father said. "That thief belonged to a dacoit subcaste, and his notorious son is alive and well. As it happens, he's a member of the Gymkhana Club in New Delhi and I can tell you he's a very vengeful fellow. He might read the passage—your books are in the club library—and kidnap Gaurev as revenge for your making public his father's seedy past."

The idea was so preposterous that I was stupefied and couldn't think of anything better to say than "Why Gaurev?"

"The thief's son lives close to Umi's house and sees Gaurev going to and coming from school every day," he said.

"Your imagination has run away with your judgment!" I cried.

"You have been out of India so long that you have lost touch," he came back. "Such primitive acts of vengeance are common in the thief subcaste, which is known for nursing revenge for generations."

I couldn't think of anything to say to dispel his fears. As absurd as I found them, I trembled slightly nonetheless. For all I knew, the thieves of the dacoit subcaste were like the Capulets. ("Daddyji" remained unaltered, and Gaurev never came to any harm.)

I had barely taken in the thief business when my father fastened on another passage in the book and charged me with unwittingly besmirching our own family's name by revealing in print that Lalaji had been a patwari—a kind of minor village official. It seemed that that petty office, always filled by Indians in the British Raj, was practically synonymous with corruption. My father was profoundly disturbed that I had made Lalaji's official position public, in case people would think that he was corrupt when he was actually completely honorable.

I protested that I had portrayed Lalaji correctly, that the British had probably put about that patwaris were corrupt because they thought all native petty officials were corrupt, and that, anyway, I doubted if any of the readers of the book would know what the reputation of a patwari was in that dim past.

My father would not be consoled. He said that at least Daulat Ram—the brother nearest his age, to whom he was closest—would know, and that he would take umbrage.

That worried me. Throughout, we had taken great care to consider the text from the point of view of the living relatives who figured in it and would read it, while at the same time being careful not to emasculate it. Although Uncle Daulat Ram's feelings were of course important to me, it was simply too late to do anything about the book.

"All this is academic," I finally said. "Even as we are talking, people are already buying and reading the book."

"But I thought the publication date wasn't for some time."

"That date is just a formality that the reviewers have to observe before they publish their reviews," I said. "The publisher ships the books to the booksellers as soon as the bound copies are ready, and a bookseller begins selling the books more or less when he receives them in his shop."

He flinched.

I realized that, by telling him the cold facts of publishing, I had administered to him stronger medicine than I had intended, and I spent the next few hours—indeed, days—alternately soothing his feelings and making him understand that the book wasn't the bomb he imagined and that, anyway, its fate was out of our hands. Fortunately, there was a hiatus of some weeks between the arrival of the first copy of the book and its formal publication, when its existence was publicized. During that time, I was able to bring my father around to accepting the book as it was. A naturally buoyant, optimistic man, he was even able to laugh at himself for his earlier sense of foreboding.

On the day of publication, however, the daily New York *Times* came out with a lukewarm review of the book, with some well-aimed barbs at my father and me. I accepted them as hazards of my chosen profession. But my father, who had no experience with the ways of the press, was outraged. As soon as he read the review, he telephoned me from 1 Fifth Avenue and complained that the reviewer had first made half a dozen factual errors in summarizing his, my father's, life and career and then, on the basis of them, proceeded to criticize him and to sit in judgment on his life.

"That's not reviewing a book but attacking my vitals," he said. He was so outraged that he wanted to go down to the paper, confront the fellow, and make him, at the least, apologize in print for his gratuitous cruelty.

I met my father for coffee and spent quite some time that morning calming him down. By the end, I thought his natural good sense had prevailed.

As it happened, that same day the book's publishers, Farrar, Straus & Giroux, were giving a publication lunch, to which they had invited fifty or sixty guests from the publishing and the literary worlds, and for which they had reserved the whole second floor of a restaurant called Lüchow's, near their offices. I wished the review had appeared a day or two later, so that it would not have taken the bloom off the party. But there was no help for it, and I got my father to promise that, whatever the provocation, he would refrain from discussing the review with anyone and that if anyone brought it up he was to feign ignorance of it.

As we were climbing the stairs at Lüchow's, we encountered the writer Isaac Bashevis Singer, and my father promptly unburdened himself to him about the review. Then, upstairs, during drinks, unbidden, he went right around the room, denouncing the review and the reviewer to anyone and everyone. "Did you see that review by Anatole Broyard in the *Times*?" he would say. "It's so inaccurate that only a cad could have written it." At the time I could have died. Now I can see his behavior in a different light; it was surely an expression of his love for me.

V

PSALMS OF PRAISES

OF YOUR FEET

S OON AFTER I RETURNED TO NEW YORK WITH THE
Red Letters in my briefcase, I was surprised to get
a letter from my father not only giving me his permission to read them but also asking for my impressions of them—though he knew full well that that
would involve the eyes of another person. Perhaps
he reasoned that that person would be in faraway
America and would have no idea who he and Rasil were and
would read the letters aloud as if they were in a storybook.
In any event, once I started reading them, with the help of
a trusted assistant, the curiosity I had felt dissipated somewhat in the face of their jarring reality. In fact, I had trouble
reading too many of them together; they gave me the dizzying
sensation of being the voyeur that I had all along dreaded
being. Their belonging to another time and generation did
not take the edge off my discomfort. Still, I couldn't stop
reading them; indeed, the story gained in intensity as I read
on, unfolding in my consciousness like a scroll, with one thing

after another opening up a new vista on Rasil's affair with my father. Some of the letters read:

MY DEAREST *MITTI* [sweetie],

> While you were here, everything was so fresh, so lively and so beautiful. Sweet, I love you with my whole heart—I feel you inside me, you are in my blood.
>
> > With many kisses
> > from your *own love.*

P.S. Since you will be staying there for a pretty long time please get yourself a smallpox vaccination.

(My father must have been on tour somewhere.)
And:

MY LIFE'S MOST EXALTED FLOWER,

> My deity, if only at this moment these love-lorn eyes could just have your *darshan* [holy audience]! If I should have your *darshan*, my heart would desire that we should get close to each other afterwards, exceedingly close, so close that we should become one so that we merge into each other, just as color dissolves in water and the two become one.

> > With Respects,
> > Your Devotee.

P.S. Varinder returned yesterday. Please excuse me writing with pencil.

And:

DEAREST,

All my time passes in *remembering* you and in *thinking* of you.

This body is yours, so is this heart,
Every single bit of me is yours,
Waking or sleeping, whatever I'm doing,
I'm always thinking of you.

God, good fortune of woman, master of forsaken ones, how handsome you are! How lovely and tender, how generous is your heart! When I think of you, it seems as if it is because of some curse in the past life, that you have been born a mortal; otherwise, your soul is that of a divine *Rishi* [hallowed sage].

I thank God greatly, who has made me worthy of your feet, and consider myself highly fortunate.

Your devotee.

And:

MY OWN DEAREST,

I have spent rather a restless night. I can't forgive myself for my misbehaviour and foolishness.

I couldn't understand what happened to me. I felt so desperate and wanted to get rid of myself—not to die, but to go away to someplace where I could meet up with nobody and where no one could see me. I believe it was the sensitivity of the mind which sometimes overpowers the person.

Imagine me kneeling down before you with folded hands, pleading for your forgiveness, for you to forget everything. I am as miserable as you must be, my darling. I did not wish to hurt your feelings—I am awfully sorry.

I am sitting in the same room where we parted, and your sweet form is before my eyes—you are sitting on the sofa and I am at your feet (the only place where I get complete peace) and your left arm is around me and your right hand on my face. How sweet you are, love.

I wonder how you passed the night; I wonder if you travelled in the same compartment with Shanti and the children.

Sweetheart, do write to me often and tell me all about yourself—how you feel and what you do.

Still another letter, which featured a pencil drawing of a woman touching a man's feet, read:

MY ALL! MY LIFE'S SUPPORT! MASTER!

Psalms of praises of your feet. You have made me wait for so long. Now, pray come soon.

Yours,
Love-lorn.

(In the British days, Biblical references were in the air.)

In other letters, Rasil dwells on her waiting to see my father, on his health, on her bouts of unnamed ailments, on their games of tennis, on her imaginings that she is getting in the way of his professional advancement, on her fears of Fatumal catching on to their affair. She talks about her daily routine: she gets up late; she takes a long time getting dressed; she looks at his picture, holds it to her heart, and kisses it; she sits on the veranda and tries to read, but turns page after page without having any idea of what she is reading; she cannot concentrate on anything for thinking of him—she sits with her sitar but cannot practice; she turns to his letters but gets so emotionally caught up in them that she can scarcely bear to read on. She tells about giving sedate purdah parties at her home for her women friends who are Muslims, and describes

going to a high-society tea at Shalimar Gardens, a Moghul
landmark in Lahore where the grandees parade on the first terrace, amid the fountains and around a large, canopied marble
throne, while the lesser notables mill around on the second
terrace—but all she can think of is what sorrows the merrymakers
are nursing and how they must be missing their own *mittis*.
When his family is visiting Lahore during some festival holi-
days in winter, she worries about his being alone in New
Delhi. She calls twice at the general post office, but finds no
letter from him. She says that when he does not take her religion seriously she is hurt. She feels his reproving letters as a
slap across her face, and his commending letters as a kiss
wiping away her tears. She compliments him for writing letters even from his sickbed. She laments her lack of sophistication in writing and her lack of formal education. At one
point, she begins signing her letters to him "wife." She casti-
gates the weather, for it either rains a lot or does not rain at
all; and it is either very cold or very hot. She excoriates the
world for giving no shelter to lovers. She thanks him for
restoring life to her when she was tired of it. She exults when
he clarifies certain misunderstandings between them. She recalls
their especially happy reunion under the full moon. She con-
gratulates him for having the rare opportunity to serve the
people, and translates some of his antituberculosis pamphlets into
Hindi. She asks him to bring back from his tour some cotton saris
with printed borders for her to play tennis in. She misses "the
spot," their secret meeting place in the hills. She sends him mes-
sages from "loneliness," "wilderness," and "dreamland"—as she
terms her long-standing states of nervous depression—and imag-
ines herself in a jungle being torn limb from limb by a tiger as
he watches. She writes about herself in the third person and con-
vinces herself that she is old, ugly, and undesirable. She adores
his figure, his complexion, his eyes, his fingers, together with
the generosity of his heart, the beauty of his soul, the grace and
gentleness of his character, the grandeur of his bearing. She
says that, in contrast, all Fatumal can lay claim to is his

wealth. She idealizes my father and denigrates herself, saying that he is as sensible as she is foolish. She consoles him for his losses in bridge by reminding him that he generally wins, and by assuring him that he will get his footing once he gets used to the new high-stakes bridge group organized by a Mr. Hayman of the Railway Board. She craves his presence. She comes down with malaria. She loses control and cries incessantly, as if she were going mad. She feels cooped up and longs to be in the jungle, calling out his name. When they meet, she wishes to kiss him first, on his forehead or on the back of his neck, as she fancies a wife would kiss her husband. She is perpetually vigilant so that their affair will not be discovered by Fatumal. She is anxious that she will not be able to have a tryst with him on his next visit to Lahore, because in Lahore, in contrast to New Delhi, or Simla, there is no obvious place that is not overrun with crowds.

Rasil complains that she has no privacy even in her house—she has to read his letters sitting on the floor in the bathroom. She worries about arousing Fatumal's suspicions—he has almost caught them together, and my father escaped detection only by hiding in the bathroom. She says that she and Fatumal scarcely speak to each other, and then only formally. She feels that Shoni, along with Pom, Nimi, and Umi, must be protected from any hint of scandal. She tells of visiting Bhabiji in Lahore. (It was eerie to see her use the same appellation for my paternal grandmother that we all did. But then I reminded myself that Rasil was regarded as family.) She spends whole days with my mother. She all but moves in with my mother in Simla, noting the daily injections and the number of pills my mother must take and what food she is able to keep down. (In Simla, my mother was subject to frequent attacks of asthma, bronchitis, and diarrhea.) She writes about going on walks with her, nursing her when she is sick in bed, reading aloud to her my father's letters to the family, and, at my mother's prompting, even writing her own distinctive letters to him. (No doubt my mother was prompting her to write letters to him either out of solicitude for him or as a way of subtly letting Rasil know that she, my mother, was aware of the affair.) When my father is away on tour, Rasil reports, in a series of letters, that my mother has bad bronchitis, has difficulty breathing, is spitting blood, and is confined to her bed. Then she says that my mother is constipated and is taking laxatives. She mentions to him the names of various doctors who should be asked to check my mother out. She expatiates on my mother's suffering. She is cheered to see my mother sitting outside. When she herself is sick, my mother visits her; Rasil finds it comforting to have my mother at her bedside. The two of them together keep the annual Karwa-chauth fast that Hindu wives keep as a mark of their sacrifice for their husbands. She feels jealous of my mother because my mother has everything that she, Rasil, would like to have, and at the same time she talks about loving my mother, not only for the fact that she belongs to him but also for herself, and loving her so much that she is prepared to sacrifice everything she wants out of life, including him, for her sake. She sympathizes with his double life—one half tranquil and happy with his family, the other half troubled and turbulent with her—and blames herself for his plight. She has bad dreams. She frets that Ravinder is putting up new obstacles to prevent her meeting my father. She is alarmed because Fatumal, having intercepted one of her letters to my father, has possibly seen through her subterfuges, and now it will be much more difficult for my father and her to carry on seeing each other.

The portrait of Rasil that emerged from her letters—a few in Hindi but most in peculiar, stilted English—was unsettling, even if fascinating. The fairy-tale creature of "Hill Girls" was shown to be a more complicated, substantive woman. On the one hand, she came across as an outgoing Western woman who played mixed tennis doubles and, on the other, as a reclusive, tormented, spiritual woman, who was no less punctilious about observing Hindu rituals than my mother. Like any subservient Hindu wife, she addressed my father as her deity and master and spoke of herself as his devotee and slave. Indeed, often her letters struck a prayerful tone, replete with a hodgepodge of allusions to the Bible and to Hindu sacred writings. As a memsahib, she might have cut a figure at the club or at the Viceregal Lodge, but underneath one sensed a childlike quality—that of the poor, shrinking hill girl she had once been. In fact, despite her attainments and superficial sophistication, she seemed to be much less mature than my mother was. Even if the personality behind the resonant words remained opaque, her letters suggested that at heart she remained a tribal girl, and so placed in doubt my father's claim about her seamless transformation from shepherdess to socialite.

I found myself asking what it was about the writer of these effusions that had entranced my father. Was it her physical appearance? But then my mother, in her own way, was extremely beautiful, too. Was it that Rasil was unfettered by the demands of children and was rich? (Shoni and Varinder were generally at boarding schools or in the care of ayahs.) But my father was a family man through and through, and he scarcely gave a thought to money, referring to it often as "the dirt that washes off hands," as if it were no more desirable and no less avoidable than common grime. Was it just sex? But the letters were nearly devoid of any explicit sexual imagery, and anyway, since the issue concerned my father, I could not pursue that line of thought very far.

I of course grasped the fervent spirit of the letters, but the more I pondered them, the more blurry their content seemed to get. But, then, they were incomplete and fragmentary. None of them had dates; some seemed to be written on the same day, others months apart; people were referred to by initials and were hardly described; and so on. Even when I was able to guess who the people were, events remained hazy. I arranged and rearranged the letters like the pieces of a jigsaw puzzle, in the hope that a chronological framework would emerge and illuminate things that were obscure, but I didn't seem to get anywhere.

I eventually wrote to my father, guardedly asking him if he could help me fill in the gaps. He responded unreservedly. I was soon drawing up lists of basic factual questions and sending them to him, along with photocopies of the letters in question for his reference. (Our understanding was that once he was done with the photocopies, he would destroy them, so that they wouldn't fall into the wrong hands.) The procedure of copies and queries was one we had long followed whenever I was writing about family matters, for which he was an incomparable source. Sometimes, when I was bombarding him with endless questions about the letters, it seemed to me as if I were trying to decipher fragments of historical documents rather than ephemeral love letters.

My father dutifully sent me the answers, if rather more slowly than with earlier projects, since, at his age—not to mention the nature of the subject—he did not find it easy to sit down to write. His answers were often accompanied by lively cover letters. "I am glad that you read the 'Red Letters' and I am glad that you found them interesting," he wrote in October of 1974, when he was nearly eighty. "I have no shyness about them because I am an objective person, an old and seasoned soldier." In December, he wrote, "I have duly received your one hundred and thirty-three questions about the Red Letters. I will try to answer them as candidly as I can." In February of the following year, he wrote, "For the last week or ten days I have been passing through a sort of mental depression. Consequently, I have not been up to answering your questions." A week later, he was counselling me to put aside autobiographical interests. "You should forget yourself for a while and blossom out in some impersonal work," he wrote, apparently forgetting that even then I was working on my book on Mahatma Gandhi. And a week later came this letter: "In attempting to answer the questions in those letters, I find myself living in the past instead of the present, which is rather annoying. After all, the past is dead and gone and the future uncertain. The present is all that counts. Sometimes I wonder if I am not accursed in having such a good memory to capture the events in such fine detail." Yet he could not put the Red Letters out of his mind any more than I could, and two days later he wrote:

> The answers I am sending you with this letter take care of all your questions. I have enjoyed the opportunity to glance through these "Red Letters" after so many years. They transported me to happy times of forty or so years ago when I was half my age.
>
> At the time I was in the prime of my life. I never knew what fear, boredom, worry, or negative thoughts were.
>
> I thought of the world as a rose garden, thorns and all. An Urdu couplet exactly expresses my thoughts and feelings at the time:
>
> > I am a worshipper of the garden but it is not
> >   only the flowers I love
> > I get along well even with the thorns.
>
> What wonderful times were those in India—in between the two World Wars, the administration moving smoothly, every wheel lubricated. Efficiency was at its best and the word corruption was not heard of in higher circles.
>
> Those six years of my life in government service spending summers in Simla, winters in New Delhi, with the whole of India as my playground, will ever remain green in my memory.

❦

IN THE PACKET of Rasil's letters, there were, surprisingly, a few letters from my father to my mother. He said he had no idea how they had got there, so I was left to speculate. Had my mother, learning of Rasil's letters, surreptitiously planted his to her among them as sort of a talisman against their continuing power over my father? That supposition wasn't as outlandish as it seemed. She could easily have discovered the cache of Red Letters, but as a traditional Hindu wife she wouldn't have dared destroy them, however much she might have wanted to.

My father's letters to my mother were dated from just after he arrived in Simla in 1931, and so they preceded his attachment to Rasil. They read rather stiffly. But then, like most couples in that period, my parents had a language problem: my mother was most comfortable reading and writing Hindi, which used the Devanagari script, but my father had trouble composing in it. The natural language for him to write a letter in was either English or Urdu, the language of instruction of his early schooling, but she couldn't read its Arabic script. She, however, had sufficient knowledge of English to be able to read simple letters in it, and that was the language he used for writing to her. Despite these hurdles, the letters had a fond ring.

Soon after he arrived in Simla in 1931, almost five and a half years to the day after their wedding, he wrote this to her in Lahore, where she was recuperating from Om's birth:

1.6.31

My dearest & sweetest Shanti,

I have received all your letters of the 27th, 29th & 30th today. I am also counting days of your arrival.

I think the best would be to come all the way to Simla by train. Let me know exactly the date & time of your arrival.

Don't forget to bring my violin & the harmonium, and bring umbrellas also, but they must be the best available.

Don't worry about the pram. I shall get you one as soon as you come.

Book as much luggage as you can through to Simla because then there would be no problem at Kalka station.

You must bring some one with you too, Lakshman, or Dwarka say, on two or three days' leave.

What about Bhabiji? Isn't she coming?

Looking forward to seeing you & the children.

> Your own darling
> Amolak

(My mother always thought that his signing his letters to her with just his first name was very Western—his full given name was Amolak Ram.)

At the time, my three older sisters and my brother were all under five, so my mother would have had trouble managing all the children on her own on the train from Lahore, especially because, to save money, they travelled in the crowded intermediate class between second and third, which, unlike the former, had no reserved seating, but which, unlike the latter, had cushions on the seats. It was advisable for one able-bodied man to accompany them, for safety and assistance. Dwarka and Lakshman were her brothers, who were extremely close to my father, and who would be able to elbow their way through the crowd, lay claim to some seats, and hold them against the onslaught of other demanding passengers until the children and my mother could be settled there.

As it turned out, my mother was not able to come as soon as planned because she came down with a fever. On the twenty-eighth of June, my father wrote:

MY DEAREST OWN,

I am very much concerned to hear that you have some fever. I am very anxious to be near you. I shall be reaching Lahore Sunday morning—I have taken one week's leave.

I have engaged a good *chaprasi* [official peon] who also knows cooking.

I'll write to you from day to day but you must stay in bed & remain quiet. [My mother, however, became so weak that my father had to drive down and bring the family up in his car.]

So far I have won over Rs500/- at bridge & have opened a separate bank account with it. They play here cash & stakes are Rs30/- per 100 points but I play only Rs5- & they carry me gladly.

With love & kisses, your own
Amolak

My father was so good at cards and so well liked that all the members of the Simla club who played bridge for high stakes were happy to "carry" him, meaning that they made up the difference between the stakes that he could afford to play for and those that they played for themselves. Consequently, they ended up subsidizing his losses but also taking the cream of his winnings. My father never worried about that—he had no interest in money. He was simply addicted to playing cards, and his friends and relatives spoke about that as his second wife.

Meanwhile, he was living in temporary lodgings while he was on the lookout for something bigger, which would comfortably accommodate the whole family. But he was having difficulty finding anything suitable for rent within his means. At one point, he thought of taking the lower flat in a cottage rented by Fatumal and Rasil. My mother was keen on the idea of living in the same house as her "blood sister." But it was not until the next summer that they were able to swing the high rent for it. In any case, it certainly did not occur to my mother that Rasil might become a rival for her husband's affection, because such affairs were scarcely known in the respected high-caste Hindu community from which my parents came. Anyway, my father's character was nothing if not steady.

❧

MY FATHER AND I had always been close and had paradoxically grown even closer since I had come to America in 1949, at the age of fifteen. Although over the years I had been able to afford to go home only infrequently, and then for brief visits, still, after the initial seven or eight years, we had managed to meet up every couple of years or so in the States, because of my father's medical assignments with Mrs. Clyde and his lecture tours. In the summer of 1975, the year after he entrusted the Red Letters to me, he was in New York and, one evening, when he was visiting me in my apartment, he asked to see the original letters. Since he had recently gone over the photocopies, I wondered why he wanted to see the originals. Was it because, having lost nearly everything in the Partition, he wanted to touch and hold practically the only surviving remnant of his personal history? Certainly, I had enjoyed handling the letters; they gave me a palpable feeling of being in contact with his past.

As I went to fetch the packet, he said over his shoulder, "Son, what did you think of them?"

"I found them somewhat cloying, especially the salutations," I said, and mentioned, as examples, "My life's most exalted flower, I bow my head before," and "My life's all, Obeisance at your feet hundreds of thousands of times."

"What can I tell you, son? That's just the nature of love letters in India."

As I gave the packet to him, the letters spilled out, falling helter-skelter on the coffee table, the sofa, and the carpet. I bent down to gather them up, and then set about trying to neaten them into some kind of order, but my father stopped me.

"These are not the kind of letters that you put in files and keep track of," he said. "They are just like fallen leaves when the autumn comes—to be raked up and chucked out, or else they will become an unholy mulch."

"As a writer, I can't take such a cavalier attitude toward any letters," I said. "I think of them rather like tea leaves that can foretell the future."

He laughed. "Old letters have nothing to do with the future, only with the past. What are you thinking of?"

"You are right," I said quickly. "I was just thinking about my own life. I have my own cache of love letters."

As soon as the words were out of my mouth, I regretted them, because I didn't want my love letters to become a subject of discussion. Fortunately, he didn't take notice of my words. Instead, he picked up an envelope, and a lock of hair dropped out. He bent down and retrieved it.

"I wonder how I missed the lock when I went through these letters before," I said.

"You probably didn't look through all the envelopes. But isn't it amazing that it has been preserved all these years?"

"Is this how you got the idea of Reshmi knitting a lock of hair into Chander's sweater?"

"No," he said, smiling. "That was another lock of Rasil's hair, but everything about the sweater, which was my favorite, was exactly as I told you. It was lost during the Partition."

He handed the lock to me. It was thick and wavy and felt almost alive. I broke out in goose bumps.

It is one thing to be told about Rasil's hair, but quite another thing to hold a lock of it in my hand, I thought. When she sent it to him, she could not have foreseen that his forty-one-year-old son would be holding it one day. I've enjoyed touching the letters, but this token of remembrance from her head is something else altogether. It's spooky.

I quickly handed the lock back to him, but he seemed to have lost interest in it, because he was already reading aloud the letter that had come with it:

I washed my hair and as I was combing it lots of hair came

off with the comb and I was so tired of its constantly falling out that I absolutely lost my temper. I seized the scissors and was just going to cut all of it off when I suddenly thought that it belongs to you. Even then, I cut a little from the top, which I am enclosing with this letter. I was sorry afterwards, and I do hope you will excuse me for this rashness.

I got up and poured him some sherry, being careful not to fill the glass too full, in case my conscience later reproached me for tempting him to divulge things he would rather not have. From the day I had got involved with the Red Letters, I felt that I was trespassing on forbidden ground, and oddly his coöperation had only heightened that feeling. I reflected that, while answering my queries about the Red Letters across the oceans over a period of several months, he might have deluded himself into believing that he was only explaining and amplifying some more of the routine matters that we often corresponded about when I was writing about my family, while in fact his explanations and amplifications succeeded only in further exposing the most intimate aspects of his life.

My father, however, now went on to read many of the other letters aloud, often laughing but sometimes also sounding as if he had a lump in his throat. Presently, he read a letter that evoked their going together to the Seepee Fair in 1931, explaining that it was held in the middle of May, in a teacup-shaped valley seven or eight miles out of Simla.

"Were Mamaji and Fatumal with you?"

"No. Om had just been born, and your mother was in Lahore, observing the tradition of a woman staying indoors for forty days after giving birth," my father said. "As for Fatumal, he must have been travelling somewhere on business. I do recall, though, that they both wrote to us encouraging us to keep each other company."

"Could a married man and a married woman step out like that?"

"The fair was in the afternoon, it was a public holiday, and it seemed perfectly natural for the two of us to go together in a rickshaw. In fact, all of Simla society, from the Viceroy to the district officer, from the Commander-in-Chief to the sublieutenant, went to the fair." He explained that the fair, originally a sort of marriage market where local adolescent tribal girls were put on show for prospective bridegrooms, had become a great Simla event, with the English sahibs and memsahibs arriving with large retinues of bearers and ayahs, syces and coolies. The officials and their families either came on horseback or were carried, along with extravagant tiffins and copious supplies, in rickshaws or jampans. The coolies, although all skin and bones, were able to pull, push, and carry huge weights, and, perhaps because they were all Pahari (hill people), they were able to climb up and down the slopes with facility that plains people simply couldn't match.

"What happened at the fair?"

"It was just a big, convivial social outing, where children rode on merry-go-rounds or a festooned elephant and watched a monkey tamasha, and the grownups wandered around stalls that sold all manner of trinkets, watched folk dances, and sat on blankets and rugs, eating their tiffin out in the open. The center of attraction was a local hill deity in the form of a mask and a covered palanquin."

So he was on an outing with a woman who he knew had been ill-used from her teens, I thought. That must have brought out his gallant side and made him feel protective toward her. That might in turn have prompted her to glorify him. Yet he must also have been under considerable constraint, thinking about Mamaji back in Lahore, in bed with Om. She had finally produced a boy after giving birth to three girls, and everyone was proud of the mother and son. Babuji was calling him the Prince of Wales.

"You already felt close to Rasil?" I asked.

"Since your mother was so close to Rasil, she was like a sister-in-law to me."

"What happened in Seepee?"

"Nothing much. We just watched the hill people dance with abandon, to the beat of drums and cymbals and maybe the air of a trumpet." He took a sip of the sherry. "I remember that Rasil, as a Pahari girl, was familiar with the dances and was tempted to join in but, mindful of her social position, held back."

He picked a letter out of the pile at random and read:

LORD OF MY LIFE,

This body, this mind, this soul—everything—even though it belongs to you—has not been of any use to you, has not been able to render you any service. This is a cause of great unhappiness to me. I can neither get a place at your blessed feet, nor live happily separated from you. I feel my ability to reason is weakening.

Master, kindly tell me which path I must take. You alone are my guru, you alone are my deity and my all.

The Khannas came over here this morning.

V. will be back either on the 13th or 14th. Do please write to me at my address.

Yours forever.

"I suppose the Khannas were Basheshwar Nath and Sheila?"

"Yes. And V. was Varinder, her younger stepson. He must have been about eleven or twelve at the time and was in Simla as a boarder at Bishop Cotton School." (Founded in 1866, the school was modelled on the public school Rugby, where the Bishop had been a pupil of the eminent headmaster Dr. Thomas Arnold.)

In my earlier, written queries, I had skirted many of the deeper issues raised by the letters, for fear of alarming him with my curiosity. Now that I was talking to him at leisure, in person, I felt free to ask him anything and everything.

"Looking through the letters, I was struck by their spiritual flavor," I said. "She talks about having your *darshan*. She addresses you worshipfully as *Rishi*. She scarcely thinks of you as mortal. I wonder why that is."

"Among Hindu women, love of a man and love of a god often get mixed up. She would say her rosary—that's what she called her Hindu prayer beads—using alternately Lord Krishna's name and my name."

"Still, her reverence for you strikes a discordant note, at least to a Western-trained ear. It seems as if she were longing not for her lover but for a deity."

"Just imagine being compared to a divine being!" He laughed, thought for a moment, and then said, "In our blessed culture, the spiritual and the sensual have always gone hand in hand."

"You mean the worship of lingam, and all that."

"Yes. You could say that spiritual reverence for a man helps a Hindu woman to feel pure as she indulges in the sensual side of life. It's all part of the complex relationship in our religion between purity and pollution. A woman dreams about making love to Krishna, the avatar of Vishnu, and she makes the man she loves into Krishna. Some Krishna devotees even believe that Krishna's illicit love for them is on a higher plane than his conjugal love for his consort, Meera, or Radha. As you know from her tattoo, Rasil had dedicated herself to Krishna. There was even something of the Christian nun in her—her extreme simplicity, her dedication, her renunciation, and her modesty. Yet, as a person, she had a formidable presence."

"Why 'formidable'?"

"Like some beautiful women, she had a deep, awesome quality, heightened by the fact that she spoke little, if at all. I remember her silence used to unnerve people, especially men. They didn't know what she was thinking—that added to her mystery. Yet with people whom she felt close to, like your dear mother and me, she behaved just like any other girl from a good family. In fact, I doubt if there were many women who were as conscientious about their family responsibilities as she was. It was heartwarming to watch her taking care of Shoni and Varinder. I daresay that people seeing Rasil and Shoni walking along the Mall in Simla would never have guessed that they were half sisters, rather than mother and daughter. I think Varinder will tell you, even today, that Rasil has always behaved toward him like a real mother. For all her sophistication, deep down she was more—more like our village women, like Bhabiji, than like the women brought up in the choked *gullis* of Lahore. She also never lost the mountain air of her childhood, and she had natural elegance of spirit. As far as I know, she never did a single mean thing."

"But what could have been meaner than to"—I searched for a word, and finally could think of nothing better than "steal you from Mamaji?"

"There you are applying your Christian, Western concepts to our Indian culture, where Hindus and Muslims have traditionally taken more than one wife. Rajas and nawabs had so many wives that they couldn't keep track of them."

I wanted to remind him that he had been incensed at the Nawab's and the Jat Raja's doings in the hills; that, anyway, we were far from being rajas and nawabs and such; that our kind had made their mark in the world by probity and respectability; and that those were the values he had brought us up with. But I checked myself. I didn't want to be or seem to be judgmental.

He happened to pick up a letter that read:

> Ravinder came at five-thirty and said to me that Varinder was arriving and that I had to go to the station with him. I think he sensed that you were coming. I pretended that I had a headache, but he wouldn't leave me alone. I went—of course Varinder wasn't at the station.
>
> Darling, I wanted to explain all of this to you this morning, but you were so angry and disbelieving that I

couldn't. I couldn't control myself long enough to say anything. Just now Shoni came to me and asked me why I was
sad. I said nothing. She sat on the bed and patted my hand.
Sweetheart, if you make me live alone in this miserable
world, I'm afraid I will kill myself.

"Kill herself? Really?" I exclaimed.

"It's just lovers' talk," he said.

"Anyway, it seems that Ravinder caught on to your
romance. How did he find out?"

"He must have guessed it."

"Did he leave her alone afterward?"

"My God, as long as I was in the picture he wouldn't
dare to touch a hair on her head. I didn't have a gun, but
he used to quake in my presence." He took another sip of
sherry.

"Do you think you got interested in her because you knew
her checkered past?"

"Well, well, well, son. We don't think like that in India.
We are ruled not by analysis, like you people in the West, but
by instinct. Still, as they say, stolen kisses are sweeter. But I
always tried not to lose my head. She, however, was swept away
by love for me."

"Were you really as rational as you now think you were?"

"The Enchanted Period, those two short years, was the
only time I have ever strayed in fifty or more years of marriage. Even then, I didn't leave my family and run away with
her, did I?"

"Yet, at one point, she starts signing her letters to you
'wife.' "

"I was certain that she knew in her heart that we could
never be married. Her signing herself 'wife' was merely an
expression of devotion."

"Yet she certainly thought that you might get married."

"What can I say, son? She and I said all kinds of things, as
people who are enamored of each other will."

"There are times when she sounds quite impulsive," I said.

"Yes, that's true, but she could also be quite sensible," he said. "Doing anything rash was never really in the cards for us. My life was my children, and she was devoted to her charges, though the last couple of months of our winter separation, when she was in Lahore and I was in Delhi, were the hardest for us, and maybe she toyed with doing all kinds of silly things."

"At one point, she was worried about being your tennis partner. Why was that? Had people started gossiping about you two?"

"We all went to the same club and played at the same tennis courts and moved in the same circle, and Simla society was so small that in the course of an afternoon you met everyone walking on the Mall, so we could never be too careful."

"How was it that you could write to each other sometimes every day and no one seemed to catch on to it?"

"Most of the time we wrote to each other care of the general post office. But, now and again, there was a letter that for some reason was urgent and had to be delivered to the house, and that's how your mother was able to steam open a letter. As you know, there is no such thing as privacy in our country."

He said that notwithstanding evidence to the contrary, Rasil loved my mother, and riffling through the pile pulled out this letter:

Ever since you left I have been worried about Shanti. Love, she is not well and she still has difficulty breathing. She spends her days in bed and she gets up in the evening and takes only a cup of milk. I spend my days with her. I try to amuse her so that she won't feel lonely. We play cards.

"And here is an even stronger illustration of her love for Shanti":

> It is for Shanti, this exceptionally sweet girl, that I am prepared to lay down all, for her, everything, my soul, my body, my flesh and all that can be dear to one I am prepared to sacrifice. She is why I can't leave *him* for you.

"I ask you if you can think of another woman, Indian or European, who would be so genuinely concerned with the welfare of another woman under the same circumstances," he said.

"Nowadays, we might say she was laying a guilt trip on Mamaji."

The concept of making someone feel worse by playing on his or her sense of having done something wrong was unfamiliar to my father, but once I explained it to him and he grasped it, he said, "I don't know if such a concept would have applied to our culture in those days. It might even be alien to it today."

"But to someone who didn't know Rasil in the way you did, her conduct toward Mamaji could have seemed somewhat hypocritical," I pressed.

"Then, do you think that I acted hypocritically also?"

I was taken aback by his question. I felt that, in answering, I had to choose between being honest, at the risk of perhaps wounding him, and being the respectful son who gave him the benefit of the doubt in everything. Eventually I said, "The behavior of any married person who is having a love affair is bound to be duplicitous. You censure Mamaji for steaming open Rasil's letter, but you also read her letter to her astrologer."

"Well, well, well. You say that you don't judge, and yet you talk like a judge."

"I don't mean to." I was afraid this was turning into an argument, so I quickly said, "As you yourself know, it is in the nature of lovers to deceive and dissemble—go through all kinds of emotional twists and turns."

❧

"RASIL SOMETIMES SOUNDS childlike in her devotion to you, a little like the way we were when we were small and thought of you as an angel and a demigod," I said on the following day, when he dropped by and settled down again with the Red Letters and a glass of sherry.

"Tell me another," he said, covering his embarrassment with laughter. "Certainly, in romance, one loses one's head and thinks all manner of fantastic thoughts."

It is ironic that my father should be telling me what romantic love is like, I thought. I have had much more experience in that department in the West than he could ever have had in India. Having left home as a boy and so having lived outside the Indian system of arranged marriages, my conscious outlook on love and marriage had become Western. But I had never shared either my ideas about such matters or, more to the point, my own romantic experiences with my father—had kept hidden from him my several searing, unrequited romantic episodes and my desire for nothing more than to get married and have children. In fact, I was so shy with him about the subject that I had nearly made it into a taboo. Not surprisingly, he therefore had no inkling of the radical changes in my thoughts and feelings about love and marriage. Did he think that my reserve was nothing more than old-fashioned Indian reticence between father and son? Did he think that I had more or less given up on love and marriage just as my cousin Vidya had when she was twelve, after her hands had become deformed as a result of tuberculosis in her wrists, and everyone had started saying she must reconcile herself to ending up as a spinster? If so, he thought of me as someone who had missed out on romance and marriage because of my blindness and yet, like Cousin Vidya, would find compensation in work and intellectual activity. But ever since he had not only allowed me to read his love letters but also talked to me openly about them, I had wished that I could be as free with him as he was free with me—reciprocate in kind, as it were. But, whatever the reason, it seemed that it was much more difficult for me to confide in him than it was for him to confide in me, and that left me feeling guilty about hugging my secrets but also feeling powerless to make a clean breast of them. Still, how I wished that I could kindle in him the hope that I stood a chance of getting married someday. So close were we emotionally that I needed him to be hopeful for me to go on hoping myself. In 1983, some eight years after this conversation, my hoping bore fruit; I got married and eventually became the father of two daughters.

"You look pensive," my father said. "Is something worrying you?"

"No," I said quickly. Even then, with all my marriage thoughts swirling in my head, I could not relax my guard and be open with him. Eventually, I said, "Reading the Red Letters all at once is overwhelming, especially because, in so many of them, Auntie Rasil seems sad and lonely even though she is madly in love."

"But she was basically a happy person," he said. "The letters might read that way because they were mostly written during the times of our separation." He sounded as if he had no doubts that he might be wrong, but then, he always emanated the self-confidence of a gambler whose bets generally paid off.

"Her letters also seem quite repetitive, as if she were a bird going round and round a cage," I said.

"After all, son, they are only love letters," he said. "Even so, as I read them, I myself find them quite different from one another."

"But, even when their content varies, they all seem to be written in the same sombre key," I said. "Of course, now and again she does strike an inspired note, but its effect is just to highlight that tone."

"What in particular are you thinking of?" he asked.

"In one letter she says, 'To me our life looks like a weak thread with knot after knot of problems.' That seems like a fairly hackneyed image, but then she does this nice turn on it: 'However one tries to untie the knots, the end of the thread does not come in sight, and there is always the fear of the thread snapping.' It is a clever way of saying that the problems of the two of you are endless and that they may overwhelm your love."

"You read these letters like a literary critic, but I have a different perspective on them. I remember how thrilled I was just to get them—just to hold them in my hand. The question of whether they were clever or simple never entered my mind."

"I also wonder about the accuracy of her perceptions. One of the 'knots' she mentions is your lack of faith and trust in her, yet everyone who comes in contact with you knows that you have the most trusting nature."

"Well, well, well, son, no love letter can stand up to your kind of close reading. Lovers have all kinds of fancies and imaginings."

"Still, her questioning your trust in her seems strange. Maybe it was just the insecurity of her position."

"I always trusted her, and she knew that. She was just anxious and worried about me."

"What 'knots' was she thinking of?"

"I would have been the last to know. But of course your dear mother was in poor health. I was trying to support four children on a government salary. Even so, I don't remember ever feeling down. I was always looking at the bright side of things. I never lost my optimism and faith in the future. The pessimism was all on Rasil's side, and it was due not so much to her nature, which was sanguine, as to her excessive anxiety. The experience of dealing with an emotionally turbulent woman has its own excitement and magic."

"I myself have been in love with some pretty difficult women," I said, trying to struggle out of my shell. "It's magical, but it can also be destructive."

"Romantic love is a terrible disease," he said. I imagined that he was so preoccupied with Rasil that he hadn't fully caught what I had said, or, more likely, I had kept him at arm's length about my romantic life for so many years that he felt apprehensive about looking too closely into it. I was relieved—it was one thing to hint at my intimate life, quite another to dwell on it.

"Why do you say that?" I asked, seizing the opportunity to turn our conversation in a more abstract direction.

"The real love of an arranged marriage is a process that grows over time, like our banyan tree, getting deeper and stronger as its branches grow downward into the ground, take root, and grow into additional trunks," he said.

From the time I was in knee pants, I had heard my father glorify the life-affirming Indian system of arranged marriage, in contrast to the morbidity of the Western system of romantic love, which, as he saw it, was based on fantasy and impulse. As a child, I couldn't imagine any system better than the one he extolled. As an adult, however, I had come to see it as a reflection of the dehumanizing effects of caste and poverty: it seemed to be based on an impersonal social and economic transaction, in which the bride and bridegroom were treated like chattel, her price being determined by her looks and her dowry, and his price by his ability to provide her with a home and financial security, to the exclusion of almost any other consideration. No doubt, my preference for romantic love over arranged marriage was in some measure colored by my having been thought all along to be a piece of damaged goods, who would therefore fare badly in the Indian marriage market.

"Your relationship with Rasil belies what you've always said about romantic love," I blurted out.

"What did you say, son?"

"When we were growing up, you used to lecture us about how the love that grows out of arranged marriage—a lifelong process—is better than the love one falls into in a headlong way. Yet what you felt for Rasil, and she for you, points to a different truth."

"Why do you say that? If I'd believed in romantic love, I would have lost my head and abandoned your dear mother and you children and run off with Rasil. As it was, I always had my feet on terra firma, and I knew where my responsibilities and obligations lay."

"But what about Rasil?"

"Because Rasil had a bad marriage, it was fortunate for her that she was a hill girl at heart."

"What does that mean?"

"Our hill girls have a romantic free spirit, not unlike your Western women. That, in Rasil's case, meant that her life was not as joyless as it otherwise could have been. But I think that, whatever Rasil might have felt, she behaved much as I did— she stayed within the fold of her family."

"But did she ever really think that you might marry her?"

"We talked about it. Lovers do. But it was just talk—a way of filling up the time and, you might say, the letters."

❦

IN ONE LETTER Rasil wrote that she had not been able to write to my father earlier because the post office was closed for the Shiite Muslim festival of Muharram, which commemorates the martyrdom of Husayn, the second son of Fatima, Muhammad's daughter. Her mention of the festival prompted me to tell my father that, when I was a child, an unthinking servant had dragged me out to the road to witness the horrifying spectacle of the mourning procession on the tenth and final day of the observances.

"I was trapped in such a dense crowd of onlookers that I couldn't move a step," I said.

"What a foolish thing for the servant to take you there!" he said. "You could have been felled by the iron chain of one of the marchers in the procession."

"I could actually hear the men marchers whacking their bare chests with chains and the women marchers pounding their breasts, all of them moaning and screaming as if they were going to die," I said.

"The marchers used to outdo one another in trying to mortify their flesh," he said. "They thought they were atoning for the martyrdom of their saint, Husayn, but it was a brutal business no matter how you looked at it. People used to faint at the sight of all that blood. We all tried to stay indoors."

"And yet, in the letter about Muharram, Rasil almost seems to identify with those self-flagellating marchers."

"There was in fact something of the martyr in her."

"Was she self-destructive, then?"

"In India, we don't go in for such fancy Western terminology."

"It's not a matter of terminology but of feelings that are universal. You'll surely agree that she often sounds depressed."

"What in particular are you thinking of?"

I mentioned a letter headed "Wilderness."

"When I received a letter from 'wilderness,' I knew that she was racked by sadness and confusion," he said. "I just took such letters as the cry of a lover."

"In such letters, she says she is too withdrawn to talk to anybody or too sad to write even to you. She often sounds tortured. Sometimes, even those letters that are brimming with affection seem joyless."

"She probably dashed off a letter in a few minutes. It captured only the mood of the moment. Love letters are by their nature fleeting and overwrought. You might say they fill in the empty spaces between partings and meetings. After she wrote a letter, her life went on in its ordinary way, and she was like any other happy society woman."

"Was that an act?"

"No, that's the way she really was, I believe. I think the unhappiness you see in the letters came from the fact that she knew from the beginning that our love was doomed. The only question was how long it could be kept going. I could always fall back on my happy family life, but she—what did she have to look forward to? Unwanted attentions from her husband and the renewal of assaults from her stepson? The tragedy of her life would melt a heart of stone."

"What about Varinder and Shoni? Did they not bring a certain happiness to her life?"

"Varinder was mostly at Bishop Cotton School, and so her only companion at home was Shoni, on whom she lavished all the love and affection for which she had no outlet in her family. That may be one reason she found so much solace in romance. Listen to this letter":

MY BEAUTIFUL DARLING,

What is love after all? To satisfy one's physical desire— that is not love. For me, love is being at one with the soul of the other. When the two souls merge—that is real and eternal love, which survives even the parting of death. If you are an idealist, then I am an idealist's wife. Love, I look to you to lift me high above the clouds and protect me from coming down to earth.

This, like so many of Rasil's other letters, was not the kind that my mother ever would—or, indeed, could—have written. Despite the outward resemblance of the two women, they were inwardly as different as a mem and a native.

VI

VACATED HOUSE

NTERSPERSED AMONG RASIL'S LETTERS TO MY
father were also, to my surprise, about ten letters
from him to her—they must have somehow escaped
the fire, and she must have returned them to him.
Reading them was much more disturbing than
reading her letters. They were as extreme as hers;
in some ways, they seemed even more extreme,
because they were free of the mishmash of Hindu senti-
ment and spiritual allusions that partially obscured the
romantic passion of hers. Having lived in the West most
of my life, I saw nothing wrong with a man bewitched, in
love, writing passionate letters—but my father? Indeed, his
letters seemed to be painfully at variance not only with the
father I had grown up with but also with the father who
had been giving me running commentary on Rasil's letters.
Had that side of him been invisible to me because I was
his son, or was it an aberration in his character, like the
Enchanted Period itself?

My dearest, my goddess [he wrote],

    Sweet, last night in the train I had a terrible longing for you. I wanted you so badly that I willed you into my dreams. In one dream, I felt your smooth body next to mine, your gentle hands touching me all over. Oh! I was so happy, so contented, so peaceful.

    Oh, how I wish you were here to see the sunset with me, saying, "Yes, it is beautiful." Life is beautiful when you are near. With love,

Your grateful darling

Sensuality was not something I associated with my high-minded father. All the same, I marvelled at his free-flowing expression of love. Feelings seemed to pour out of him like water from a pitcher. Even though I was a writer, when I sat down to write a love letter I froze. I couldn't work out why I was so cautious, so held in, so wary—even to someone I loved.

Sweetheart [he wrote],

    Darling, as I told you, I read the same satirical article about love as you did. But what does Jean Barlow, the writer, know of love? She has never fallen in love. She sings the praises of friendship—who would deny that? She talks about thoughtfulness, consideration, and loyalty amongst friends. Of course these are wonderful qualities, and are equally essential between lovers. But friendship is only the younger sister of love. Lovers sacrifice everything—friends do not. Lovers are prepared to live or die together—friends are not. I quite agree with her that love brings unhappiness but there is charm in that. The heart-beats of lovers, their sensations, their sorrows, their pleasures, the true happiness lovers experience for a few moments is enough of a compensation for all the unhappiness.

Friendship is beautiful and may or may not be between persons of the same sex. But love is always ripe in persons of opposite sexes. As friends we have so much in common— the sports, the mental outlook on life, generosity of spirit, love for the jungle, the fresh air, the hills, the mountains and the rivers and complete lack of love for money.

The day after tomorrow I am off on a long, long tour— alone. By God, I hate to live without you. When I am travelling, I sometimes wish to jump out of the window to cut out the misery of living without you.

> With love and kisses,
> *Your own.*

It was touching to see him dismiss the critics of romantic love and accept even its unhappiness.

DEAREST SWEETEST LOVE,

Before I met you I would have agreed with every word in that article satirizing romantic love, I scorned love, I laughed at it, I pitied those who loved. I believe I told you as much. But since then I could not live a day without your love.

By all means play in that tennis tournament because you know you will win and you might regret not having played in it.

For my part, I never regret anything, nor forget anything. I take everything seriously. I suffer things patiently, silently, and bear life philosophically. In fact, I'm a lone wolf. You are the only person to whom I have opened my heart.

I fear I have lost self-control and have been writing far too often. It is like this—I keep on thinking of you day and night, I keep on dreaming of you, I keep on reading your letters. I keep on singing to you and then I can't help writing to you. But I shall try not to write too often. The rest I can't help.

I live in memories, in dreams, in reveries, in idealism. Goodbye, sweet, and good luck.

Love and kisses all over from
Your own

It seemed to me that this letter, written some forty years earlier, had a contemporary, universal ring and revealed my father to have a young heart and insouciant character. Still, it was a far cry from all his discourses on the virtues of arranged marriage that we had been treated to when we were growing up. Those discourses might have been the result of his mature reflection after he had been ambushed by romantic love. Still, his once having championed it and been wounded by it made me feel closer to him, for he was voicing some of my own thoughts when I myself had been in love.

Another letter read:

SWEETEST LOVE, MY OWN,

So that loafer called on you. Oh, how that makes my blood boil. What right had he? He may be a rich fellow, well-placed, a member of the Cosmopolitan Club, but he is a cad. I knew after he met my sweetheart he would speak ill of you. The wretch—I hate him as much as you do, if not more.

I am too upset to write any more—my pen is going dry. More when we meet.

Your own

There was a hint of Victorian melodrama in the rhetoric of the letter, as if he had been influenced by readings in that genre about "cads" and "swells." Also, jealousy and hatred were not emotions I had ever known my father to express, so I asked him about the so-called cad, and he said, "Fatumal was using his wife to ingratiate himself with a Sindhi government officer by the name of Hiro from whom he wanted some business favors. Fatumal put Rasil in the officer's way, as if as a husband he had the right to offer her to him, and got Hiro to invite them to Karachi, where the fellow had a seaside home, for their Christmas holiday. Fatumal was delighted to take his holiday on the Arabian Sea. But after the officer tried to get what he thought was his due from Rasil and she rejected him violently, he started speaking ill of her, as if she had duped him, when in fact she was blameless. I tried to console her as best I could, but, with Fatumal as her husband, her life was always a bed of nails, so to speak. There were times when she couldn't stand being near him—the very sight of him would make her shiver."

MY DEAREST AND PRECIOUS JEWEL,

Darling, as always, two contradictory thoughts crossed my mind: (1) A great desire to be one with you—in this I lose my sense of reason and ask myself, "What am I here for? Why can't I be with her?" and so on, which makes me feel sick of life and so utterly depressed; (2) I feel sorry for others and hate myself for being an intruder in your marriage. Then I am reasonable and can see things through and think things out.

Your own
Devotee

The contradiction between passion and reason which he describes was inherent in his situation. He couldn't renounce her, but he also realized the compromising moral situation in which he found himself. But, whatever the power of his emotional involvement, when it came to the crunch, and he had to choose between Rasil and my mother, all along he must have known at some level what he would do, just as he said. Indeed, I ascribed his depression and his sense of futility to his knowledge from the outset that his love for Rasil could meet with no other fate than slow death. Such feelings were exacerbated by the vagaries of sending and receiving letters—with perhaps the post office misplacing them.

SWEETEST,

Apparently you did not get my letter. It broke my heart when I learnt of it because darling, in that letter I had expressed my feelings of the two missed evenings. I had expressed my agony at your tears, tears of which I was the cause. Love, how can I atone for those tears? I assure you when I saw you, with your eyes tinged red, I felt utterly miserable. Why I allowed you to cry I'll never understand and why I did not take you in my arms and kiss those tears away shows how helpless I felt.

I also wrote you letters from Loneliness, Wilderness, and Dreamland but you don't seem to have gotten them either.

[He broke into Urdu] "Woe on such a life,
you somewhere else and I somewhere else."

But yet I go on living because you want me to live. I go on trying to be philosophic, but I often feel "What's the use?"

I feel that your state of mind is just the same as mine because we always think alike.

Sweetheart, you have set such a high standard of love and purity and devotion that I am engrossed by the thought of you all the time, and the world appears barren and deserted without you.

Sweet if you can't come in person do keep on sending mind waves. Perhaps without heartache life is not worth living.

[Again in Urdu] "One who has given me heartache
May God bless him/her."

> God bless you sweet,
> With love and kisses all over,
> From your
> Own for ever

His letters had all the marks of those of star-crossed lovers.
Suicide hovered over them, not so much as an actual possibility
but as a dark shadow. He wrote:

MY DARLING,

I wish you knew how I feel when you are not near me.
I feel incomplete—my throat dries up, my chest feels
hollow, and I get a sinking feeling in my heart. My very soul
seems to be missing.

Oh! I wish you were here to embrace and kiss me. Then
I would feel whole and strong.

Oh! don't go, please don't! Then I might do something
rash and you will be sorry.

> I am, always,
> Your own.

He struck an even more deeply melancholic note in the following letter:

DEAREST SWEETEST LOVE,

I wonder if you have ever realised how miserably and
sadly I pass these days. Each and every moment is vacant,
absolutely nothing, just a *living death* without you. I am
alone all the time—half the time I'm traveling and have
no company, the other half, I don't want company, just

want to be alone with my thoughts, and the thoughts are full of you.

Sweet, those journeys and visits to the "spot"s, those rainy nights, those early mornings, those drives and kisses—these are food for my soul, as well as my thoughts. Without them, I would have been dead by now. In fact, without you, I prefer death to life. My sorrow is that I can't make you mine, with just you and me and no one else in the world.

Life holds nothing for me if you are not there. I am desperate and I may do something Rash, but I can't decide what I should do. A Rash act would make you look back on those good old days and miss me. Though I want you to miss me, I wish to be able to see you whenever you want me and when I can. If I went away for good and you were unable to forget me, my soul would not be at rest and I would haunt your dreams. If you are even half as much in love as I am, or even one-tenth saturated with thoughts and memories as I am, then you can't forget me, you cannot have peace without me.

His wish for release in death might be nothing more than a lover's fantasy—you'll really miss me when I'm gone! But the idea that my father should have ever thought that life was not worth living was unsettling. It was so contrary to the way I'd always thought of him—a cheerful, upbeat person, who always saw the best in everything and everyone, and who, unlike anyone else I'd ever known, believed there was nothing I couldn't do. When we were children, if one of us happened to be in a depressed mood, he would say, "What is a mood? It's just your imagining." No matter how depressed I felt inside, I had always tried to emulate his optimistic, buoyant nature. But this letter made me realize that he was subject to drastic swings of emotion himself, had even at least one time been desperately depressed. The realization had the contradictory effects of making me feel closer to him and of liberating me from his shadow—all part of my belated growing up.

The letter closed, "With thousand kisses and embraces for my love. Your slave in exile. Being in exile—such is my lot." His closing echoed in a momentary way my own lifelong exile with respect to anything and everything. My father had spent nearly all his life in India and was firmly rooted in Indian traditions and the Indian way of thinking. Consequently, I had always assumed that, given my long years of exile in the West, he could not understand certain things about me. But in the letter he came across as an Englishman of Raj vintage. Indeed, I now wondered if his romance with Rasil was part of his romance with England, which had long predated and was to long outlast the Enchanted Period. Anyway, he showed himself as someone who could look beyond his own culture—step out of it and adopt a whole different identity, like the novelist that he had fantasized about becoming. He was nothing if not versatile, with a great capacity for living and dreaming.

❦

FROM MY OWN experiences of falling in love, I knew all too well what it was like to pine after a sweetheart—to long for the touch of her hand, for a kiss from her lips, for the feel of her breath. Sometimes, my yearning would reach such a fever, would be so desperate and overwhelming that I could scarcely be still—could not sit, stand, or even lie down. Indeed, when I was in the throes of love, the loss of my sense of self was so complete that I lived almost only in the reflection of my sweetheart—thinking that if it faded I would fade with it. But, sooner or later, the world would intrude on our love, bringing in its wake mundane demands and obligations and the general pressures of surviving. Something similar happened in my father's two remaining letters. The reality of his impossible situation with Rasil seemed to assert itself. Although there appeared to be no dampening of their passion, their trysts seemed to fall off, and the fear that their relationship would become public seemed to press upon them.

SWEETHEART,

No news from you. I leave for the next town in the tour tomorrow morning. Oh God, why can't I instead fly back to the loving arms and the warm bosom of my sweetest girl? Why did you make me give you up forever?

Love, I have tried to obey you & keep Shanti happy. But I can't do it. I want you *alone*—otherwise I am afraid I can have no peace of mind.

I hope I will hear from you one day as you promised. I trust you so. I only wish you knew what consolation & peace I used to get when I received your letters. How my heart would beat and what delicious sensations I used to get.

Darling, what will I do now—how will I bear life without your letters! I am so silly writing this way when I know you will never read this letter & will never even know that I wrote. I am mad. Why do I go on writing? Perhaps you too are thinking of me and writing to me at this time.

Yes I live in hope.

> With thousand kisses & love
> From your
> Devoted slave

In the other letter he wrote:

DEAREST ONE,

How sorry I was to see you driving round and round my house last night. For a moment I felt like jumping in your motorcar, putting my arms around you and kissing you. But darling, you know the world in which we live. We cannot defy it. Since we have to live in this world we must avoid giving other people cause to think badly of us. There was a time when I didn't give a damn about them—you were the only one in the world who mattered. Since then I have lived through many ups and downs, which has brought me back to my senses. I have become so wary, that before I take a step, I think, "What will Shanti's people say, what will my people say, what will everyone think, and if your feelings towards me should change (after all, we are all human) what will I do then?" I know that to think all of this is absurd, but I can't help it. . . . So many silly thoughts come to mind that I become confused. Sometimes my head is full of nonsense and sometimes it is empty like a vacated house. You can help me to sort through them. I need to talk to you. I love you purely and devotedly. Every part of my body, heart and soul, word and deed, is yours. Yet Love, when we are together, I feel we are not one. Something in you or me keeps us apart—but sweet, in saying this I mean to give no offense. I have always been true and faithful to you and shall always remain the same.

As he sensed, they could not defy the world for long, and his feeling that his mind was like a vacated house was itself an omen.

❧

SOMETIME IN THE autumn of 1933, the second year of the Enchanted Period, my father, mistakenly thinking that Fatumal was out of station, sent a letter to Rasil not in care of the general post office as usual but to her house in Lahore. Fatumal intercepted the letter and opened it. Until then, he had apparently had no suspicion about Rasil's entanglement with my father. What exactly Fatumal did when confronted with the evidence of the affair my father never knew, because Rasil turned away all his inquiries with what my father called her Mona Lisa smile. She either did not want to make trouble between the two men or she thought it best to deal with Fatumal on her own. My father, however, presumed that Fatumal got even with her in some underhanded way but did not physically mistreat her. Fatumal was always mindful that his position in both Lahore and Simla societies was precarious and depended mainly upon Rasil. Certainly, my father did not notice any change in Fatumal's behavior toward him.

In December, not long after Rasil drove "round and round" my father's house in New Delhi and he restrained himself from going out to her, he came down with a mysterious illness. It was never diagnosed definitively, but it was so serious that he was forced to take a long leave from his Simla-Delhi job and to move to Babuji and Mataji's house in Lahore. He was confined to his bed for nearly three months and, sometimes, he was so sick that he was delirious, even talking about Rasil in his sleep, much to the consternation of my mother.

However Rasil might have wanted to see him, for the sake of propriety she mostly kept away, writing little and scarcely calling at 16 Mozang Road to find out how he was doing, as many friends did. It seemed that Fatumal was keeping close tabs on Rasil and that she was no longer free to do what she liked. Still, when she heard that my father's life was endangered by the sickness, she wrote to him secretly:

> There is a saying that the mullah's run extends no further than the mosque. Similarly, my run extends no further than praying to God, "O God! If I love him truly with all my heart, then pray remove his troubles and sorrows and adorn him with happiness."

In point of fact, the conditions of their lives had already begun to pull them apart, and prayers were about all either of them could venture for the other.

In March of 1934, around the time of my birth, my father began to rally slowly. Throughout, everyone had ascribed his illness to his exhausting work in the two capitals and to his late nights at card tables. My mother had privately also ascribed it to the strain of his leading a double life. Both he and Rasil now took his illness as a timely warning. They had all along known that his conflict could not be resolved in her favor—that, as a devoted family man, he could not leave his wife and children and that, as a government officer, he had to uphold a certain standard of rectitude. Despite that, they had trouble completely breaking off writing or seeing each other, so the question of their future relationship remained in abeyance when he resumed his duties in Simla that April.

He and the family had hardly settled in Simla when he heard of a position with better prospects in Calcutta, as assistant to a Colonel Stewart, a professor at the recently founded All-India Institute of Hygiene and Public Health Administration. My mother and Babuji hinted that moving to Calcutta might be the best thing he could do, because that would put a long geographical distance between him and Rasil. Indeed, he himself thought that that would perhaps help him finally disengage himself from her, as well as being the best step for his career. He arranged to stay in Calcutta with a classfellow from Government College, Dr. Ram Bihar Lal, and took the 1,170-mile train journey out there. He was interviewed for and was offered the job, but, the evening after, he happened to run into a friend from the Punjab, Colonel Sir Ramnath Chopra, the director of the School for Tropical Medicine in Calcutta, who said that in fact Colonel Stewart was not going to retire until he had to, so that my father, if he took the position of assistant, would be stuck in it indefinitely. Sir Ramnath added that Calcutta's climate and water did not suit Punjabis and that his own health and that of his family had broken down since he had moved there. As if Sir Ramnath's arguments were not compelling enough, my father found his resolve to terminate his relationship with Rasil weakening. He declined the position. But he always wondered whether, by not moving to Calcutta, he had missed a great opportunity to enter the international academic world at a young age.

❧

WHILE MY FATHER was in Calcutta, he had left my mother and us children in the care of our maternal great-grandmother Manji and our uncle Dwarka, both of whom were staying with our family in Simla. He had been gone a few days when Uncle Dwarka ran up to my mother holding a telegram.

At the sight of the telegram, my mother took alarm. The baby sock she was knitting for me dropped from her hands. She started to wheeze, and her chest began to heave and rattle.

"Is Doctor Sahib dead? What's happened?" She heard, as if from far away, Uncle Dwarka reading the telegram from my father: "PLEASE SEND SHANTI TO CALCUTTA STOP NOT TAKING JOB BUT RETURN DELAYED STOP."

My mother was convinced that my father would never have asked for her to come, with all the children on her hands and just after her forty-day confinement following my birth, unless he had suffered a serious relapse. Even as she busied herself in getting ready for the long journey, she fretted whether she would ever see my father's face again.

On the evening that Uncle Dwarka received my father's telegram, he brought all of us down from Simla on the narrow-gauge train to Kalka. There, he put my mother and me on a train bound for Calcutta, gave my mother her ticket, placed her bedroll, tiffin carrier, and thermos next to her on the seat in the ladies' compartment, and wished her a good journey. After that, he put everyone else—Manji, my sisters, Om—on another train, bound for Lahore, and returned to Simla to keep an eye on the empty cottage.

My mother had never taken such a long train journey— one whole day and night and then some, to the other side of the subcontinent. She was so afraid of the dacoits who were known to waylay trains and rob the women passengers of their jewelry and finery, and even beat and murder them, that she shut and locked the door of the compartment tight, opening it only when she was certain that a lady passenger was trying to get in. She herself did not stir out of the compartment. On the journey, she prayed and breast-fed me on schedule. She often held her breath to ward off an asthmatic attack and staved off hunger by eating whatever she had been able to fit into the tiffin carrier, washing the food down with milk from the thermos.

As the train was pulling into the station in Calcutta, she spotted on the platform the wife of Dr. Lal. My mother let down the window of the compartment and called out, "You come with news from Doctor Sahib? What's happened to him? Where is he?"

Mrs. Lal, an energetic, agreeable woman, ran alongside the slowing train, calling back reassurances. The station was so huge, noisy, and confusing that my mother felt dazed and over-whelmed. Mrs. Lal took me from my mother's arms, grasped my mother's hand, and nodded firmly to a coolie to pick up the luggage and follow. "There's nothing, absolutely nothing, to be alarmed about," Mrs. Lal said as they were walking out of the station. "He developed a fever soon after the interview and had to be taken to the hospital. I feel terrible that he got the fever under our roof."

Outside the station, Mrs. Lal hailed a carriage, put us in, and got in after us. My mother insisted on going straight to the hospital, and Mrs. Lal dropped her there and took me and the luggage home with her.

My father lay in a bright-white hospital room. He slept so heavily that, even when my mother entered, he didn't wake up. She drew a chair next to his bed and sat patiently, either crying or talking to the nurses. He woke a few times, recognized her and took notice of her presence, and then immediately fell back to sleep.

In the evening, Dr. Lal took her home. There, she and Mrs. Lal cooked a lot of halvah and puris, rounded up twenty Brahmans from neighboring *gullis*, and fed them all their stomachs could hold. The Brahmans assured the women that God just then was receptive to acts of charity and that Doctor Sahib's fever would soon be gone—and indeed it was, the very next day. The diagnosis in Calcutta was no more conclusive than that in Lahore, but he was well on his way to full recovery.

That summer, Fatumal took Rasil to Kashmir instead of Simla. Whatever her inclinations, there was no question of Rasil's protesting or going against his wishes. The husband's word was law in Indian marriages.

Given the smallness of Lahore and Simla society, whatever the private inclinations of Rasil and my father, they had no choice but to try to maintain some kind of friendship, through letters and occasionally seeing each other socially. In one letter, he had begged her to tell him how he should conduct himself without her, and she wrote:

> You asked me, Love, to guide you and show you the light. You might just as well have asked the glow-worm to show the light to the moon. But since you so desire, I will tell you one thing. Never lose your self-respect and pride, and you shall be very happy.

With their love affair closed and sealed, almost like a forgotten letter, she now wrote to him with such formality that it was hard to imagine that he had ever been anything to her. She wrote this to him in 1936:

MY DEAREST FRIEND,

> No news from you. I hope you are keeping well. Please send me Krishan's address, will you? [Krishan had joined the army.]

How is Shanti keeping? I wrote two letters to her but have received no reply. Did you receive my last letter?

> With all good wishes
> Your ever friend

In 1937, my father, having grown disillusioned with some of his British colleagues, resigned from his Simla-Delhi job and took six months' leave in England, to which he was entitled. After that, he returned to his department in Lahore. Now if he saw Rasil at all it was only in social situations.

❧

"Before I came to New York, your dear mother and I dined with Varinder and his wife in New Delhi," my father said when he was visiting in 1975. "They live in a mansion of a house, which they built after the Partition. He has felt attached to me since he was a boy, because I helped him enter the Indian Military Academy in Dehra Dun. He went on to have a distinguished career in the army, and recently retired with the rank of major general. He and his wife never had children, but his wife has made quite a hobby of collecting cut-glass curios."

How Indian of him to keep in touch with the stepson and the daughter-in-law of his former paramour, I thought. "What ever happened to Fatumal?"

"Around the time we left Simla, Fatumal bought Rachel's Folly, a lovely, palatial establishment considered one of the most valuable properties in Simla, and he and Rasil starting living there more or less year-round. But a couple of years later he was indicted for cheating the government out of big sums of money and put in jail. Before bail could be arranged, he tore the sheet off his bed, made it into a rope, climbed up onto a chair, tied one end of the rope to the ceiling-fan hook and the other end around his neck, and kicked the chair out from under him."

"What a terrible death!"

"The poor fellow had nothing but unhappiness in his life, even though he valiantly tried to make the best of it," my father said. "The only thing in which he could rightfully take pride was his adoption of Shoni."

"I remember her slightly from when we were growing up."

"A couple of years after Fatumal died, Shoni eloped with a top cricket player. The first I heard about it was when Rasil rang me up at the office. She was distraught and had turned to me as a last resort. She wanted me to find out if the fellow was of age; otherwise, she was going to send the police after him. She seemed to think that boys underage could not run off and get married. I didn't know what the law was, but when I checked his college records, I discovered that he was of age. There was nothing she could do, therefore. Within a year or so, the couple got formally married. They eventually had two children, but the marriage didn't last. Rasil brought up one of the children as her own, exactly as she had brought up Shoni."

"And Ravinder—whatever happened to him?"

"In 1930, he had got himself a good job as an electrical engineer in Delhi and found himself a pretty, well-educated girl for a wife. Her complexion was so fair and his so dark that they were known in the club as White and Black, as Rasil and Fatumal were in their time. They had three children, and I think that Ravinder was a good father—or, at least, so it was said. But his was not a happy marriage. In the late thirties, the couple separated. His wife, who kept the children, became a devotee of Sai Baba—a saintly fellow with a long flowing beard—while Ravinder went back to Simla. His living in Rachel's Folly with Fatumal and Rasil might have started out as a convenience. But, once Fatumal died, one thing led to another, and Ravinder and Rasil were soon living as husband and wife."

"Her stepson and rapist, living with her as an illicit husband—how sordid!" I exclaimed. "Did she capitulate to him because he supported her financially?"

"Oh, no, no, no. Quite the contrary, she supported him—Fatumal had left her plenty of money. Even if he hadn't, Rachel's Folly had become such a valuable piece of property that she could have rented it out, even off-season, and that in itself would have brought her enough income to live anywhere like a maharani."

"Then how would you explain their ending up together?" I asked.

"I can't," he said. "All I can think of is that, from the beginning, she had exerted a great pull on Ravinder, and though no one, least of all me, could have suspected it at the time, he must have exerted some pull on her, too. After all, he had forced himself on her for years before I came into the picture. Who's to say? Once Fatumal and Ravinder's wife were out of the way, they must have been both lonely, though living under the same roof. Becoming a full-fledged couple might then have been the most convenient arrangement for each of them."

"Still, it all seems so sordid. And she seems to have been so refined and religious. It doesn't make sense."

"She was certainly refined, but she was also a tribal hill girl, and tribal people are generally freer about such things. In the hills, all manner of things go on that cannot be done in the plains without terrible consequences."

"They must have travelled as a couple to the plains, and all the servants and callers must have known, and so on," I said. "The stepmother and stepson living together must have created quite a scandal."

"Respectability is everything for government servants and middle-class people. But rich people are a law unto themselves. Anyway, Rasil and Ravinder mostly lived in total seclusion in Rachel's Folly, guarded all the time by ferocious Alsatian dogs. One approached the cottage only at one's peril. In fact, she completely withdrew from society. She never came to any club, she never picked up a tennis racquet, she never made a fourth at a bridge table. If they went to the plains, it was generally

Allahabad, where Ravinder had some property, in a part of the country where no one knew anything of their past."

"But so many people had known her in the plains—in Lahore and in Delhi—and God knows where else. They must have gossiped about them."

"No doubt. But they began their life together at the height of the Second World War. After that, the British left, and there was the Partition and the diaspora. The society scattered to the different corners of India. The whole tenor of life changed. No one cared about who had cut a great figure in Simla in the good old days. Those kinds of things don't get into the history books.

"Are Ravinder and Rasil still among the living?" I asked.

"Very much so. They still share Rachel's Folly, but people say that lately she has become as chaste as a nun, devoting herself completely to Lord Krishna, her first love, and praying night and day to a small ivory statue of the deity playing the flute—you know, the kind you can buy in any bazaar. In time, she has completely given herself over to idolatry and Hindu mythology. In or out of season, she stays in Simla, inside Rachel's Folly, and doesn't even come out for a stroll along the Mall, something everyone still does, morning and evening. But whenever she goes to Allahabad she stops in Delhi to see Shoni or Varinder. We run into her every year or two. Our meetings are always friendly. Recently, your dear mother and I called at Varinder's house, and she was there. She had in her arms Shoni's infant grandson, which reminded me how she loved children. That was, after all, what had originally drawn your dear mother to her."

In 2000, Rasil died when she was a month short of her hundredth birthday.

VII

THE LONG-LIVED

ONE

A S A SMALL CHILD, I AM TOLD, I WAS UNCOMMONLY
attached to my mother. But as I grew older what I
wanted most was schooling, something denied to me
because no one in India seemed to know how to teach
more than rudiments to a blind child. I therefore came
to identify more with my father than with my mother,
because he believed in science and education. He flatly
repudiated astrology and self-styled gurus of any kind, while
she, otherwise a rational and competent woman, dreaded certain conjunctions of the stars. She would even be convinced
something awful was going to happen if she broke a mirror or
encountered a black cat. Her superstition was one of my conscious causes for my turning away from her. Still, in retrospect,
I sometimes wonder if her asthmatic attacks, to which she had
been subject daily for as long as I could remember, had been
even more decisive in alienating me from her. I remember
being terribly upset by her loud, labored breathing and her
wheezing, her spasms of coughing, hacking, and spitting—all

the more so because I relied on sound to orient myself and to get around and my hearing was so acute that even the crackling of a newspaper or a shopping bag got on my nerves. Her asthmatic sounds were so much a part of her that I could scarcely think of her without thinking of them. Yet she had a great sense of humor and laughed easily, even uproariously. In fact, the house was generally filled with the sounds of her talking and laughing, humming and singing, as she went about her daily chores.

Even as my heart went out to her during an attack, I wanted to bolt at the first sign of it. Instead, I would stand around, terrified that she might not be able to catch her next breath. Indeed, she would often cry out, between strangled breaths, "I'm going. . . . This time I'm really going." We children would gather around her, feeling helpless and saying repeatedly, "Don't go. . . . Please don't leave us, Mamaji," as if our incantations had the power to stop her attack. In such an emergency, I would become my superstitious mother's son, praying to God to make our incantations work, like the proverbial atheist in a foxhole.

I recall a particular emergency. It was after the Partition and at the time of our stay in Simla. I happened to be alone with my mother in Erneston. My father had gone away on a tour of a refugee camp; our servant, Gian Chand, had taken my little sister and brother out for a walk; and my older sisters and Om had gone to the top of Tara Devi, a local hill, to have a picnic. I had wanted to go with the older children, but they wouldn't take me, because they said I wasn't a "grownup." I was thirteen, neither still a boy nor yet a man.

I had barely stopped crying out of disappointment at that when a Dr. Kapur arrived at our cottage to give my mother a liver-extract injection for anemia. Besides being asthmatic, she tended to be anemic, perhaps because she had given birth to eight children. In any event, she seemed always to be in indifferent health, and one doctor or another was always paying a house call.

I stood around while Dr. Kapur sterilized a needle on a

portable stove in the room where Mamaji lay, filling the air with the familiar smell of burning paraffin. After he had given her the injection, he went on his way. But when he had been gone only a few minutes my mother's breathing became fitful and noisy. She complained of stiffness in her joints, moaning that she could not sit up, or even turn on her side.

"I'm going, youngster," she said in a choked voice. "This time, I'm really going."

Flailing my arms helplessly and shouting wildly, "Help! Help! My mother is dying!," I ran out of the cottage and up the slope of the ravine to the road. By an extraordinary coincidence, I bumped into one of my father's dispensary assistants, who was stepping along to an appointment. I cried out, "Mamaji got a bad liver injection! She's dying!"

He rushed down with me to the cottage and gave my mother another injection.

His intervention apparently countered an allergic reaction to the earlier injection, because my mother rallied at once. (My father later said that, if his dispensary assistant had not had his medical bag with him and had not had the presence of mind to act quickly, she could have died from anaphylactic shock.)

"I knew all along, youngster, that Ram had brought you into the world to save your mother's life," she said to me, adding, with a laugh, "If you do nothing else in this world, you have earned so much credit with this deed that when you grow up you will ride a blue horse." A blue horse was a symbol of the advent of great riches.

I savored for a moment the pleasure of having taken part in saving my mother's life. But then I remembered that I had run up onto the road driven not only by the impulse to help her but also by the panicked wish to get away.

❧

I RECALL THAT, when we were children, my father used to say that my mother's asthma was not hereditary, since no one

else in her family had it. It had developed out of a case of
bronchitis that had permanently affected her lungs, he
thus, it had an ostensible medical cause. But he also tho
that it was psychosomatic in origin, perhaps the result of s
deep-seated, unconscious fear. He felt that, if she could bi
that fear out into the open and spit it out, so to speak,
might be rid of her asthma once and for all.

Then I learned, at some point during our talk about tl
Red Letters, that she had contracted the bronchitis in 193
when the family had first moved to Simla. It had no
responded to any known medicine (at the time, antibiotics
had not yet come to India). Within a few weeks it had meta-
morphosed into asthma. Doctors ascribed her illness to Simla's
climate—to the fog and mist, and to the deluge of monsoon
rains. The damp air and dense forest were a lethal combina-
tion for all kinds of respiratory diseases and allergies. My
father, like the English Simla residents, thrived in the climate. For him, it was reminiscent of London. But my mother
was laid low by it. She had the tropical heat in her bones,
and she used to say that she constantly shivered in Simla,
that—no matter how many warm woollen vests, sweaters, and
socks she put on—she could never seem to get warm. Of
course, there were many sunny days in the rainy season, but
she used to say that her memory of Simla was dominated by
the wet cold.

Almost from the moment my father told me about the
chronology of his dalliance, I began wondering about the connection between it and my mother's illness. Right after my
mother came up to Simla for the first time, Rasil had practically moved into the flat to nurse her and Om. Soon, she had
generally taken charge of my sisters and the servants. My
mother had embraced her as a sister, but she could also have
felt jealous of her, in that she was able to do everything my
mother was unable to at the time because of her poor health. A
year later, the Enchanted Period had begun. I imagined that
she might have been driven half out of her mind by the idea of

her husband running off with Rasil, but could find no outlet for her feelings, and so had literally choked on them. Whatever reassurances he might have given her about his permanent commitment to her and his children could have made little difference. Indeed, her frustration could have manifested itself in asthmatic attacks; in that case, I felt, they must have come to her as a relief, even as they frightened us children about the possibility of losing her. She was perhaps as frightened about losing our father.

When I asked my father about the connection between Rasil and my mother's asthma, he first flatly denied it. He pointed out that the asthma predated his affair with Rasil. Later, he equivocated, and allowed that it might have been exacerbated by the affair, adding, "The connection you speak of never struck me. I always had the impression that she knew I would never leave her."

"Maybe at a conscious level she did know that, but at an unconscious level?" I asked.

"I never gave that much thought," he said.

"If your running away with Rasil was the deep-seated, unconscious fear you referred to, do you think that her talking about it might help her get rid of her asthma?"

"Oh my God, all that happened so long ago. There is now such a long history to her asthma that, sad to say, I don't think she can ever be free of it."

"What about psychotherapy?" I knew that the question was absurd in my mother's context, but I threw it out anyway.

He laughed. "In India it is thought of as a Western form of astrology, if anyone has heard of it there at all."

I got his point and dropped the subject.

All the same, I recalled that, as I was growing up, my mother, generally an equable, affectionate, and, on the whole, cheerful woman, was sometimes given to fits of rage. Then whoever happened to be near her would catch it. She would slap us children across the face so hard that our cheeks would

smart. As soon as her rage subsided, she would be all remorse and sweetness. Once I learned about the Red Letters, I began wondering if my mother's rage might be connected with my father's romance, like her asthma—if the romance, even though finished and done with, had continued to haunt her. I conjectured that my mother, helpless in the face of my father's infidelity, might have bottled up her rage, only to have it periodically erupt without her having any control over it. I even felt that the consequences of my father's dalliance on my mother might have extended to me in my adult life, since I had already decided that her capricious behavior when I was growing up had interfered with my own ability to build a full life for myself. Certainly, in the years when all my friends were getting married and raising children I was stuck in the sterile life of a bachelor. If I courted a woman, she turned out to be capricious; if I found a stable woman, I turned away from her, fearing that she would end up being capricious, like my mother.

The implication of such an interpretation was so chilling that I could scarcely entertain it. It went against everything I ever thought about my father: I had always imagined that he had been born without the darkness that shadowed the lives of us lesser mortals. His charm and warmth, his nobility and generosity of spirit—his appreciation of people irrespective of who they were and what walk of life they hailed from—were evident to all who came in contact with him, even casually. In fact, everyone who met him regarded him as his or her best friend. Now I sometimes wished I had never heard of the Red Letters and wondered if it was the pressure of his advancing years that had made him disclose to me his romance with Rasil, without being aware of the earthquake it would cause in my soul. As a result, I would now have to obsessively mull over the whole Rasil business. In time, I would get over my shock, see him in a gentler light, and, what was even more important, see my mother in a gentler light and feel emotionally still closer to her than I consciously remembered feeling as a boy. I would then tell myself that, thanks to the Red Letters, my picture of my parents had become more mature, not to mention more complete, yet there would always remain a residue of sadness, even mourning, for my innocence before my knowledge of the Red Letters.

❧

SINCE COMING TO America, I had seen scarcely anything of my mother. Her visits to the West were rare, and my visits home were infrequent, because, living by my pen, I was often in straitened circumstances. Even when we did meet, it was always for a brief time, and we could not think of much to say to each other. Although in some part of my mind I went on feeling emotionally close to her, our experiences of the world were so different that we seemed to have little common ground. After I came to the West, I had not even been able to keep in touch with her through letters. Generally, I had no one around who could read Hindi, and although in conversation there was no one in our family who was better than she was at little observations, full of humor, about people and places, she had never learned to express herself on paper. Her letters of necessity tended to be formulaic, with admonitions encouraging me to do well in my studies or my work and to look after my health, together with invocations of a panoply of Hindu gods. When we did meet, she hardly ever talked about her past. Indeed, as a person she was more opaque, and less accessible, than my father.

For some time, whenever I visited New Delhi I would take desultory notes for a biographical portrait of my mother, a companion volume to "Daddyji." Not only did I want to redress the balance, but I also wanted to get to know her history as well as I knew my father's. Indeed, I dreamt of making the portraits of my parents into the foundation of that much larger and much more ambitious literary work, almost Proustian in scale. In fact, I imagined that my mother's story might turn out to be even more revealing than that of my father. Certainly, writing about her would present me with more challenges than usual, since, among other things, it would require me to step into a woman's consciousness.

I had not been able to make much headway in my efforts to draw my mother out. She told me point-blank that there was nothing of interest in her life, and the project had languished. But I was not one to give up easily, and when my father had returned to New Delhi after my talks with him about the Red Letters in New York, I wrote to him, asking him to see if he could make any progress in getting her to talk. He wrote back:

> I have been trying to draw out of Shanti some of her recollections of her childhood, etc., but it has been a wild goose chase. She completely withdraws into her shell and nothing much can be done about it. You might remember the review of "Daddyji" in the *New York Times* in which the reviewer rightly stressed the point that what, after all, was the importance of the subject of your father to the general public. To you, of course, the subject was important, and so was the rise and fall and rise again of your ancestors and family. It also may be that your capturing in "Daddyji" your family's life in the nineteenth- and twentieth-century is a page of contemporary history and therefore has some value. But what I am trying to impress upon you is that a book about your mother would achieve nothing, apart from washing dirty linen in public, as she says. I would very strongly urge you to go into the realm of fiction rather than biographical sketches.

Contrary to the contention of Broyard, the *Times* reviewer, I believed that the story of any person, however insignificant and humble, had intrinsic value—that the more specifically individual the story, the more universally general it was. What was the stuff of literature if not individual stories? And whether it was fact or fiction seemed to me to be less important than the content and its presentation. As for going into the "realm of fiction," I had already ventured there and produced a book, and would do so again, but my interest in writing my mother's story did not preclude that. I wrote to my father telling him all this and asking him to try again. He replied, "I am afraid you will not get any recountable episodes from Shanti's life; these were, to say the least, tragic; she was just a victim of circumstances. Her father remained self-centered and selfish, and her mother a suffering and self-effacing martyr who did not get any peace of mind. I am mentioning this to you for whatever it is worth. Of course, you can keep on trying your mother if you so desire."

"Victim," "martyr," "tragic" episodes—what were they if not the great stuff of literature? He was intending to put me off my mother's story by reciting his familiar complaints, especially about his father-in-law, Babuji, but it had the reverse effect. I felt that my father was just too different from Babuji and too biassed against him to be able to take a correct measure.

It occurred to me that if I could get my mother to London for a vacation, away from India and Indian attitudes about a woman's deferring to her husband in everything, I might be able to get her to talk. But the mere idea of being alone with her made me apprehensive. What would we do when I wasn't talking to her for the book, I wondered. How would we get through the day? Would she irritate me, as she had when I was a child, with her clumsy but well-meaning attempts to relate to my blindness? As best as I could remember, she had never emotionally accepted the fact of my blindness; she had clung to a fantasy that my sight would be restored one day.

I broached the idea of the London vacation to my parents. Given the kind of marriage they had, there was no way to get her out without him. "We would of course love to be in London with you, but I warn you that you won't have any better luck in London than we have had here," my father wrote from New Delhi. "You will only be moving the venue of your wild goose chase." I said I would take my chances; I had felt that I had no choice but to try to talk to her ever since I discovered the existence of the Red Letters, a couple of years earlier now. Through an advertisement in the London *Times*, I rented an inexpensive house out of central London, sight unseen, from a schoolteacher, and flew them and myself over for a fortnight's stay. That was all I could afford.

The moment my mother walked into the house, she nearly fainted at the dirt and the clutter and started wheezing from the thick layers of dust coating everything. "*Hare Ram, hare Ram*, I've never seen such a messy house, and I've seen some of the poorest hovels in India!" she exclaimed, between choked breaths. She couldn't believe that anyone, especially an English person, could live in such squalor. We discovered from pictures, children's books, and other paraphernalia around the house that its owner was a single mother with several children.

"The poor woman is probably so caught up in her work and children that she has no time even to sleep," my father said.

My mother was somewhat mollified, but she refused to unpack until we had all gone to a housewares store, bought mops, brooms, buckets, and dusters, and she had given the kitchen and a couple of bedrooms a once-over, so that we could at least camp out there.

I had made a condition with my father that he would not be present when I was talking to my mother for the book, so during the day he wandered around the parks and squares of his beloved London and dropped by his old haunts, like the Library of the British Medical Association. Meanwhile, my mother and I talked, holed up in the kitchen. It was a family joke that she could never sit still or keep her hands unoccupied, and she was constantly getting up to make tea, to get something to knit, sew, or mend, or to fetch an inhaler for her asthma. But once she started talking, there was no stopping her. It seemed that, all her adult life, while she might have demurely deferred to my father about what she felt and thought, she had been quietly storing up events and incidents, and now that she had the chance to tell her story, it came bubbling out of her like agitated champagne from an overchilled bottle. Like that of any mother of many demanding children, her attention span was short, and something was always reminding her of something else. She would also often begin an anecdote or an episode from the middle or the end and tell it in a helter-skelter manner. But her stories were always animated by wonderfully detailed observations and piquant perceptions. Equally impressive, everything she said was laced with humor, as if laughter had been her way of coping with the trials of life. Indeed, she had learned to see comedy even in tragedy.

During one of our conversations, my mother said, "I am as much Babuji's daughter as the wife of the Long-Lived One, and the relationship between the two exalted ones was difficult from the start. Each fancied himself a raja, and you know what rajas are like. They don't mind what goes on behind their back, but in front of them what they like to hear is 'Yes, sir! . . . Yes, sir!' Now, you've heard your daddy say Babuji should have made sure that I had a bachelor of arts. You tell me, youngster, can a bachelor of arts by itself make babies, wash their nappies, see them through diphtheria and a hundred other heartaches?" She erupted in laughter, wheezing and half choking on the tea she was drinking. "Your daddy says that he was cheated into marrying me by a couple of matchmakers, but he was England-returned and thirty-one years old. How could a mere matchmaker lead him by the nose? Anyway, your daddy doesn't deny that the matchmakers were acting on their own, not on Babuji's say-so. Besides, did the Long-Lived One ever tell Babuji that he wanted a bachelor of arts who could *toon-toon* in English and chirp like a songbird? If he had, Babuji would have told Doctor Sahib to get a mem and a radio. Your daddy says he should have interviewed me, and then he would have found out for himself that I wasn't well schooled, like the wife of his English dreams. Young people nowadays might go in for interviews and whiling away time with each other in coffeehouses before they tie the knot, but, in those days, a boy was lucky if he got a chance to glimpse a girl's face before he married her. The Long-Lived One caught sight of my face and he fell for me. You tell me, youngster, was that my fault? Was that Babuji's fault? It was Doctor Sahib's own wish and desire to have me. I tell you, he couldn't wait to jump up onto the wedding mare and carry me off. The Long-Lived One says that as soon as he talked to me on our wedding night his hopes were dashed. Maybe so—who am I to contradict the Long-Lived One?—but in those early years no one listening to him singing to me and whispering endearments would ever have thought that. In fact, Doctor Sahib used to go around his club and office saying he had a queen for a wife. Doctor Sahib might have forgotten, but I cannot forget. Whatever the Long-Lived One might say now, in those days no daughters of Punjabi notables went to college. He tells you children now about his regret for the wife he didn't find. I just listen to such stories quietly and laugh inside. As your daddy says, 'laugh and the world laughs with you. Cry, and you cry alone.' Anyway, as I tell myself, 'who's ever heard of a raja being argued out of his dreams?' If the dreams give the Long-Lived One amusement and diversion, who am I to complain? But I'd like you, youngster, to tell me which woman could have got through the good and bad times with him with unfailing good cheer. Which Indian mem could have stuck around to bear and raise his seven children and hear about his huge bridge and poker losses without so much as one squeak of protest, while serving him hand and foot? He would come home and say, 'Shanti, today I'm down blank thousands of rupees.' I might faint inside—that might be many times his year's salary, or the price of all my jewelry, or perhaps even of our house—but I would put up a brave face and say, 'What does it matter? As you say, "money comes, money goes." You'll win it all back tomorrow.' He would say,

'What if I don't?' I would say, 'The goddess Lakshmi has always smiled upon you. Why would she suddenly stop?' If he'd got himself an Indian mem, she would have taken fright at his losses and flown away. At the first sign of difficulty, she would say"—here my mother broke into English—"'Nice to know you, thank you very much.' She would wave her dainty hand and say, 'Ta-ta,' and prance off. Youngster, I'll tell you something I've never told anyone. He never wanted an educated wife. His own mother, Bhabiji, was not educated. None of his sisters-in-law were. Like me, they were brought up to sew, knit, and mend clothes, and manage children and a household. Now, your Auntie Rasil was everything he said he wanted in a wife. She could play tennis like a mem, she could play bridge like an ultramodern woman, and she could *toon-toon* in English. Yet she walked and talked exactly like me. In dress and habits, in her tastes in food, in her yearnings she was no different from me. So what was the reason for his running after her like a shikari? I ask God, what misdeeds had I committed in my previous incarnations to put the trial of Rasil in my path? But even when that trial was sprung on me I did not lose my courage. I solved that problem, like all the other thorny problems which God saw fit to lay upon me, with good humor and good cheer. And Doctor Sahib would be the first one to admit that your Auntie Rasil was better as a dalliance than a homemaker. Well, he had his dalliance. She came like a butterfly and went away like a butterfly, while I lumbered on like a faithful mule. The Long-Lived One only had to walk into a room for all the butterflies to flock to him like milkmaids to Lord Krishna. Now, Babuji—he was different. He could not charm people with smiles and Western knowledge as the Long-Lived One did without trying. He won arguments in the court of law and on his veranda. He inspired fear with his stick. And which Mehta could stand up to the Long-Lived One the way Babuji could? There you have the source of their trouble. Both were born suns, in their own right. But the temper of the Mehtas is a whole other subject. We Mehras were so well brought-up that when we felt our temper rising we bit our tongue and pushed it down, but not so the Mehtas. They are real demons. Your daddy talks you children's ears off about how the Mehtas come from a stronger village stock, are bold, and roll over all obstacles like juggernauts, while we Mehras are closed-in city and *gulli* people, are ruled by fear, and fall over with the touch of a finger, like a house of cards. I've been hearing him say such things for years. But I ask you, youngster, except for Doctor Sahib, which of the Mehtas could have touched the hem of Babuji's dress coat? Which one of them could have been an advocate on the Punjab High Court and a syndic of Punjab University, like Babuji? You children grew up saying you are Mehtas, but you are just as much Mehras—of course you are sons and daughters of your daddy, but you're just as much grandsons and granddaughters of Babuji."

I listened to my mother, savoring the irony that I had had to bring her all the way to London to discover her Indian past. At the same time, I was mesmerized by her inimitable voice and her matchless views and impressions, all the more forceful and urgent for having been kept in check for so long. Within the space of our short stay in London, I had gathered enough material to start constructing a book about her. With the aid of private diaries and letters and of public records, I spent the next two years in New York writing the book. Although I knew about the Red Letters, I could not so much as mention them, because I was under my father's injunction to make sure that no one in the world knew about them as long as he and my mother were alive. Consequently, in the book, which was published as "Mamaji," in 1979, I carefully skirted my father's love affair and portrayed Rasil and Fatumal the way I had perceived them before I learned about the Red Letters—simply as close friends of my parents.

EPILOGUE

TERMINABLE AND INTERMINABLE

I N THE NINETEEN-SEVENTIES, I HAD GONE IN FOR psychoanalysis in New York with a distinguished Hungarian doctor, Robert (Robi) Bak, a large man with a big ego. I had once owned up to him that I sometimes wished I had gone for my analysis to K. R. (Kurt) Eissler, who was reputed to be the last of the Freudian giants. Bak had said, in his customary ironic way, "So you think I'm second-rate." His remark had perhaps been intended to squelch my wish, but I had told him that I still regretted not having gone to Eissler and that he shouldn't feel slighted. He knew as well as I that Eissler, the Viennese founder and keeper of the Freud Archives, was so closely identified with the father of psychoanalysis that some people thought that going to him was almost like going to Freud himself. Bak had laughed and made fun of my wanting to go to Freud's ostensible surrogate, saying, "You'd rather sit at the feet of a great thinker and scholar up in some tower and listen to his great pronouncements than come here to me for grubby analytic work." I had said, "That's right." He had said, "I think we should analyze why you are drawn to an ascetic, lonely man." I had said, "Is Eissler really ascetic and lonely, like a monk?" Bak had not deigned to satisfy my curiosity. Instead, he had said, "We should analyze if there's something in your character that always has to have the best—the best university to study at, the best magazine to write for, even the best tailor to fit you up with clothes. Perhaps you feel damaged because of your blindness and you want to compensate for it by thinking you are getting the best." I had said, "Do you really think that's true?" He had said, "Maybe yes, maybe no." I had told him that he and his "maybe yes, maybe no" interpretations often reminded me of an old song that my father used to sing:

> There's a fruitshop down our street,
> It's run by a Greek,
> And he sells good things to eat,
> You should hear him speak
> When you ask him anything
> He never answers "No"
> He just yesses you to death
> And as he takes your dough he tells you:
> "Yes! We have no bananas.
> We have no bananas today."

Bak, always one to want to have the last word, had said, "We should analyze why you think of me as a Greek banana seller."

In the middle of my analysis, Bak died, and I finished with a successor analyst. Still, now and again, I would catch myself wondering what it would really have been like to have gone to Eissler, as if the choice of one's analyst were as prey to the ambiguity of "maybe yes, maybe no" as anything else in life.

Then, on July 26, 1986, my father died, at the age of almost ninety-one. I was wracked with grief, but tears wouldn't come to my eyes. I wondered if my ability to experience a

whole range of emotions—one of the fruits of my psychoanalysis—had suddenly become impaired. I thought that
Eissler might help me to unblock my emotions and to come
to terms with my incomparable loss. But I felt ashamed about
going back, as it were, to a school from which I had long since
graduated. But then I recalled that Freud, confronting a central question of analysis, whether it was "terminable" or "interminable," had written: "Every analyst should periodically—at
intervals of five years or so—submit himself to analysis once
more, without feeling ashamed of taking this step. This
would mean, then, that not only the therapeutic analysis of
patients but his own analysis would change from a terminable into an interminable task." I reasoned that, if ana-
lysts could go back for a brushup course without shame, then
so could I. I got in touch with Eissler and made an appointment to see him for two or three sessions. What follows is a
distilled version of them.

❧

EISSLER HAD HIS office in his residence on Ninetieth Street
and Central Park West, in a large apartment building called,
interestingly, El Dorado. Feeling anything but a conquistador
in search of the land of desire, I followed the analysand's routine, in which I was well-versed from my time with Bak, of
stealing into the doctor's waiting room. I rang the doorbell just
long enough to announce my arrival; stepped through the
unlocked door into the hall; and walked into the waiting room,
which, instead of a door, had a heavy curtain, as in some European houses. Although I parted the curtain just enough to pass
through, nonetheless the metal rings on the curtain rod rattled
in the stillness, grating on my nerves. All around was the comforting smell of old books and sweet tobacco, which seemed to
have settled into the furniture and become a permanent part of
the ambience of the place.

I sat down, with my back to the curtain, in one of several

old, capacious easy chairs, with strips of polished wood set in the armrests so that the fabric would not get soiled by sweaty hands. Through the window, which I faced, came the slight rumble of the Central Park West traffic eight floors below.

I heard the door of Eissler's private office open, rapid footsteps, and the banging of the front door—the familiar signals of a previous patient's departure. My heart began to race. Even though I had trained myself to voice my most private thoughts and feelings to a psychoanalyst—the sine qua non of treatment—still I suddenly felt small and apprehensive at the thought of mentally undressing myself, as it were, to yet another doctor.

I almost jumped up as the curtain was pulled aside and a kind voice from somewhere over my head said, "Yes, sir." It was Dr. Eissler.

I'm a patient and he calls me sir, I thought. What is his fantasy? That the formal suit I am dressed in is a form of analytic defense? That my clothes close me off from life? That I am trying to hide something? I dismissed such concerns as inappropriate, since Eissler had the reputation of being so formal and old-fashioned that he hardly ever called his friends or colleagues by their first names and himself liked them to call him Eissler.

He led the way into his office, with a slow, wobbly gait, shuffling along, scarcely lifting his feet. He was seventy-eight years old. He sat down behind his desk, and I drew up a chair across from him.

"Yes, sir," he said again, leaning forward.

"My father died a few months ago, in July."

"Yes?"

"When I got the news, I felt devastated, but my eyes wouldn't tear. You probably think that I think it's unmanly to cry. That's not so. When a woman I loved abandoned me, I cried for months on end. Whenever I hear the marriage vows at someone's wedding, I get a lump in my throat, and my eyes tear. When I saw 'The Diary of Anne Frank,' I embarrassed everyone with me because I couldn't control my crying at the end. I can't work out why the tears wouldn't come to me at the news of my father's death."

"Why does that worry you?"

"I was closer to him than to anyone else in the world. With him gone, the world suddenly seems emptier and lonelier. I feel like an orphan."

"Your mother predeceased him?"

"Oh, no. She's very much around. But for more than thirty-seven years I've lived in the West, away from her."

"Your father was in the West with you?"

"Oh, no. But in recent years he was able to visit here every year or two for a few weeks."

"You said goodbye to your father? You were at his bedside?"

"I could have been with him, but I wasn't—that's the awful thing. I knew he was weak and ailing, and I even worried about him dying. In fact, I was planning to go to New Delhi a few weeks later, in August. I was looking forward to my wife, Linn, getting to know my family better, and I wanted to show off Sage, my first child, who was twenty months old—especially to my father, who had seen her only once before, when she was just a small baby. Who knew how long he would be around? You see, I didn't get married until I was forty-nine and didn't have my daughter until I was fifty. I should have gone in July, the moment I heard that he was in danger, but having got married so recently, I couldn't tear myself away from my family. I was also racing to finish 'The Stolen Light,' my new book, before my amanuensis was due to leave, in August."

"Are you that dependent on an amanuensis?"

"She had been with me for a year, and bringing in someone new, at that stage of the book, would have been disruptive."

"But you knew he was sick?"

"He wasn't sick as such. He had fallen and broken his hip. The doctors didn't want to risk operating on him—he was over ninety and a heart patient. But, as he saw it, it was a choice of either taking the risk or being bedridden for the rest of his life. He thought that was no choice, so he ordered the doctors to operate."

"Ordered them?"

"He was a very senior doctor, and no one in the Delhi medical community dared refuse him. He was operated on by the best surgeon there."

"And you didn't go home for his operation?"

"I telephoned a week or so before it. My father, my mother, my sisters all came on the telephone and said that there was no reason for me to change my plans and fly home earlier. They all assured me that he was in no imminent danger. My father's voice sounded strong. In fact, he seemed to be in good spirits and said that he would surprise everyone by pulling through the operation and living for a long time."

"You believed all those reassurances, knowing that he had a weak heart and was that old?"

"I shouldn't have, but I did."

"You wanted to believe them?"

"I suppose. If it had been just me, I would have flown over as soon as I heard about the operation, but, as it was, it involved Linn and Sage, and I didn't want to disrupt our arrangements."

"Could you have gone by yourself and let them follow you later?"

"Yes. But, having got married so late in the day, I couldn't bear the idea of being separated from them."

"And it was inconvenient for you to go because of your book?"

"Yes. But the truth is, at the time I could no more imagine my father's dying than I could imagine my not being born. That might sound to you like a hyperbole, but that's the way I felt."

"Your father died during the operation?"

"No. He came out of the anesthesia completely conscious and in command of himself, even though he knew that he was about to die. He congratulated the doctors gathered around his bed for having done an excellent job, shook hands with each of them, said his final goodbyes to the family members in the room, and then closed his eyes and dropped off to sleep. Within an hour or two, he was dead. When I later saw my mother in India, she told me, 'He died like a lion, just as he had lived—with strength and dignity.'"

"You got there for his funeral and said your goodbyes to him that way?"

"There was no chance for that. He was cremated within hours. In India, the traditional final rites are generally performed quickly. There are certain rites that are performed later, like taking the 'flowers'—the bones—for immersion in the sacred rivers, and having a religious ceremony at home on the fourth and thirteenth day after the death. But, having missed his death, I saw no point in rushing there for them."

"Isn't honoring the dead part of your tradition?"

"It is, but I'd much rather deal with grief in private than in a public ceremony."

"Still, the ceremonies were for your father. I'm sure you would have done anything for him. Was it too much hassle for you to go all the way to India to honor him?"

"That could be. I would have had to rush there without my wife and daughter."

"So what did you do?"

"I finished my book and went in August with my family, as we had planned."

"I mean, what did you do when you got the news of his death?"

"He died on a Saturday, and we were in Cooperstown for the weekend. The town has no direct train or plane access, so I wasn't even able to get back to Manhattan to be alone with my grief."

"You didn't want to be with your new family at such a time?"

"It wasn't just Linn and Sage I was with—that would have been all right—but we were staying with Linn's mother. Her uncle and aunt also have houses there. None of them really knew my father to any extent to speak of."

"You spent the day with Linn?"

"Well, Linn didn't know my father all that well. I had an overwhelming feeling of inertia, so I threw myself into activity, which is what I always do to ward off depression. I busied myself trying to get my father a respectable obituary in the newspapers. That seemed to me to be about the only thing I could now do for him."

"Did you succeed?"

"Far beyond my expectations. There were lead obituaries in New York and London and other obituaries were carried on a wire service, something quite extraordinary, since he was not an international figure. The family in India was pleased."

❧

"DID YOUR FATHER ever cry?" Eissler asked now.

"I remember him telling me that he cried like a child when his father died," I said, "and there were so many family tragedies that he could never get over. Whenever he remembered his youngest brother, Krishan, tears would come to his eyes—Krishan had been bayoneted to death by the Japanese in the Second World War. He cried uncontrollably when my oldest sister, Pom, who had two healthy children, carried a baby boy to full term only to have its heart stop just before delivery. This happened not once but three times. Then, in 1978, her husband, Kakaji, who was only sixty years old but had begun to lose his memory and his mind, immolated himself. My father sobbed and sobbed. He couldn't get over the manner of Kakaji's death and its devastating effect on Pom and their two children. It was also especially galling to him that his oldest son-in-law, whom he had chosen with great care for his eldest daughter, should have predeceased him."

"You were with him all those times when he was sobbing and crying?"

"Of course, I was not at home when any of these tragedies occurred. But whenever I met up with him he had only to remember Krishan or Kakaji or Pom's stillborn babies, and he would get teary. But the only time I myself ever witnessed him sobbing uncontrollably was when he was seventy-two and he was having dinner at my apartment in New York. I was giving a party for him and my mother, who for once had come out to the States. I wanted them to meet William Shawn, my editor, who was the most important person in my life in America, and his family—I'd become close to all of them. I imagined that my father would be happy seeing me established in my own little home, with my friends. I felt I had fulfilled all his hopes for me and shaken free of the shackles of my blindness. Instead, in the middle of the party, he broke down and started crying, saying that he felt responsible for my having gone blind. I was mortified. One moment, I was sailing high and feeling proud. The next moment, I was drowning, totally humiliated."

"Why did he feel guilty?"

"He said that if he hadn't delayed the diagnosis and treatment of my meningitis to keep an appointment to play tennis with his visiting superior, my eyes might have been saved."

"Did you agree with him?"

"There was nothing to agree or disagree with. As I saw it, he was talking about might-have-beens. That was no more fruitful than my idly wondering what would have happened if I had married Mary, a college sweetheart I was in love with thirty years ago. That kind of parlor game, I'm sure, we can all play ad infinitum."

As if stabbed by a sharp pain, I was reminded of my father's love letters, which I hadn't thought about or looked at since those days, in 1975, when my father was in New York and we had looked through them together.

"You are silent—what are you thinking about?"

"My father had a paramour," I blurted out. "Her name was Rasil."

"Yes?"

"His romance was brief, less than two years long, and was the only time he ever strayed in sixty-one years of loving marriage, but I feel it had a terrible effect on my mother."

"Not on you?"

"That all happened before I was born, and I was forty years old when I learnt about the affair."

"Is it the effect on your mother that you want to talk about?"

"Oh, no. That's a whole different story. The reason I'm here is that I can't cry—cry for my father."

❧

"I CAN'T IMAGINE there could be any connection between my knowledge about the Red Letters and my not being able to cry over my father's death," I said at another session. "Can you?"

"Based on what you've told me about the Red Letters, my hunch would be that there is no connection between them and what you perceive as your inadequate reaction to your father's death, because you describe your father's romance without sounding judgmental or angry."

"Do you then think my reaction to his death was inadequate?"

"I wouldn't think so. Clearly, you felt extremely sad. You are still grieving and mourning for him. You simply didn't have a physical manifestation of your grief. Anyway, what is there in crying? Crying in and of itself is not a sign of emotional health. Many people can cry on demand. You recall Hamlet's speech about the actor in the Players scene: 'Tears in his eyes, distraction in 's aspect, / A broken voice, and his whole function suiting / With forms to his conceit? And all for nothing! / For Hecuba! / What's Hecuba to him or he to Hecuba / That he should weep for her?'"

"But ever since our last session, I've been thinking again about the Red Letters. I carry them around in my head like a ball of guilty knowledge. I wish I'd never heard of them. I don't know what to do with this knowledge. It's so complicated, so touching, and so dark. It has just occurred to me that his guilt over my blindness might be a cover for his guilt over his Enchanted Period!" I checked myself—I was beginning to sound unhinged.

"Are you thinking of writing about all this?"

"I want to."

"What is stopping you? After all, you are a writer."

Suddenly, I found myself sobbing. Tears streamed out of my eyes. My nose started dripping, embarrassingly.

He handed me some tissues, which he seemed to have at the ready. I wiped my eyes and blew my nose, but the tears would not stop.

"I'm sorry," I said, through my tears.

"Please feel free to cry."

"But I didn't cry when I got the news."

"When you cry is not as important as that you are able to cry."

As I left Eissler's office, I felt united with my father, through our longest-delayed tears. Although shed for reasons of our own, which even we might not have known for certain, they provided us with a connective release from guilty burdens.

AFTERWORD

S INCE 1971, BETWEEN WRITING OTHER BOOKS, I'VE
been working on a series of connected but independent volumes under the omnibus title Continents
of Exile, of which this is the eleventh and last book.
The series is predicated on the notion that the more
particular a story, the more universal it is; and thus
although the work is ostensibly autobiographical, it
tells a cross-cultural story of India, England, and America. At
the same time, it is also an intellectual voyage, which explores
themes of family and love, journalism and psychoanalysis,
among others. The story itself spans the twentieth century,
with parts of it reaching back to the nineteenth.

The narrative had its modest beginnings in family stories
my father used to tell us children when we were small. Later,
when I started writing them down, they grew as if by their own
momentum until—contrary to the spirit of free association—
they eventually acquired a distinct design and architecture.
Along the way, though, I periodically asked myself, "How can

anyone be expected to read so much about one life?" The answer, of course, is that since Continents is by tradition a saga, it relates the stories of hundreds of lives, with characters appearing and reappearing from book to book, and with me serving as a sort of narrative thread.

Insofar as Continents belongs to any genre, it belongs to the literature of exile, for in the series I try to touch the limits of time and memory across lost space, and use the persona of the narrator as a means of studying a variety of relationships. Although each book is self-contained in its chronological framework, so that it can be read without reference to its predecessors or its successors, the books taken together are a single work, the whole being greater than the sum of its parts. And although the story explores the labyrinth of subjective experiences, its tone is objective, focussing on the principal action, in order to fasten on the heart of a memory.

The inspiration for Continents of Exile was the epic works of Proust and Joyce—but my approach, from the very start, was different. The ground for Continents was broken in "Face to Face," my first book, most of which was written when I was twenty. When I wrote that book, not only was my grasp of English weak but also some of my richest emotional and intellectual experiences—at Oxford and Harvard, in New York and on *The New Yorker*, with my wife and my children—were in the future. Moreover, in that book I relied completely on my memory to construct a chronological story. My work in Continents is also constructed from memory but is buttressed by interviews, letters, diaries, wills, land deeds, books, and newspaper articles. In other words, I have relied on an armature of fact, much as many modern writers have availed themselves of myth. I was trained as a historian but ended up as a writer, one discipline reinforcing the other. In Continents I employ such fictional devices as flashback and flash-forward, description and narration, together with such nonfictional techniques as interviewing the cast of characters whenever I can. In this way, I check my recollection against theirs and, when necessary, assimilate their memories into mine and into the text itself, in the hope of making my account accurate—faithful to the spirit of what actually happened. This method of extensively mining the memories of others is, I believe, unique to this autobiography, as is my attempt as a blind narrator to re-create the visual world in what are nonfictional works. As far as I am aware, no writer has tried to do this in books that are not fiction or poetry, and how and why I do it is a subtext of "All For Love" (2001), the ninth book in Continents.

Each book in the series is organized around a central metaphor, so that while it has a basis in chronological reality, and tells the story from the narrator's perspective during the period being described, the import of the book is also symbolic: "Daddyji" (1972), a cornerstone of the series and a biographical portrait of my father, is set in the nineteenth and twentieth centuries and is, by extension, the story of an ancient Hindu family from an Indian village, aspiring to enter the modern world. "Mamaji" (1979), the other cornerstone and a biographical portrait of my mother, is again set in the nineteenth and twentieth centuries; it, too, is by extension the story of an ancient Hindu family, but this time from an Indian city, and this time not so much aspiring to enter the modern world as attempting to consolidate its place in that world. "Vedi" (1982) is the story of my stay, far from home, from ages five to eight, at a Christian missionary orphanage-cum-school for the blind in Bombay. How I ended up and survived there is the subject of the book. In planning it, I had imagined those years would be a chapter in a larger book, but as I started writing and thinking about the experience my memory expanded, by a process of association, to encompass more and more material. (I finally spent two years writing about those three childhood years.) Not only does the book recount my early experiences but it also, by analogy, tells of the world of childhood and, perhaps, the schooling of blind children anywhere. "The Ledge Between the Streams" (1984) is, at one level, a story of the convergent influences of a Hindu orthodox mother and a Western-trained doctor on one of their children and, at another, a story of the bloody Partition of the country of my birth, which laid waste the innocence of childhood itself for a generation. "Sound-Shadows of the New World" (1986) is an exploration not only of my adolescence in Arkansas but also of my discovery of education and liberation in the new country as a mid-century immigrant. "The Stolen Light" (1989), an account of my gaining academic and sexual knowledge in California, is also a social history of the American fifties. "Up at Oxford" (1993) is about the fulfillment of a dream—of acquiring intellectual prowess, and of winning acceptance—but it is also a salute to an ancient seat of learning. "Remembering Mr. Shawn's *New Yorker*" (1998), a portrait of my relationship with my American mentor, is a story of that great literary and journalistic institution under Shawn's leadership. "All for Love," which tells of my journey through the fog of romantic relationships, is also a look into the workings of psychoanalysis. "Dark Harbor" (2003), a comedy of social and architectural imbroglios, is about creating a home and family late in life. This book—concerning, as it does, the relationships between father and son and between fact and fiction—casts a backward glance on the whole series, putting "Daddyji" in a new light and thereby, even as it shifts the perspective on everything that has gone before, bringing the Continents story full circle.